MAN OF
VALOR,
MAN OF
GRACE

MAN OF
VALOR,
MAN OF
GRACE

CHARLES R. SWINDOLL

NELSON
BOOKS
An Imprint of Thomas Nelson

CONTENTS

INTRODUCTION

A Man Worth Measuring

About a century ago, as poet and historian Carl Sandburg was finishing his multivolume biography of Abraham Lincoln, he was searching for an appropriate title of the seventy-fifth chapter, which covered events immediately following Lincoln's assassination. Sandburg settled on a quaint old woodsman's proverb: "A tree is best measured when it's down." In Sandburg's opinion, not until a life is "down" can we adequately measure its significance, its breadth of impact, its depth of character.

That's equally true of a once great king named David. The only person in all of Scripture to be called "a man after God's own heart," David is mentioned in the New Testament more often than any other Old Testament character. Poet, musician, courageous warrior, and national statesman, David distinguished himself as one of God's greatest men. In battle, he modeled invincible confidence. In decisions, he judged with wisdom and equity. In loneliness, he wrote with transparent vulnerability and quiet trust. In friendship, he was loyal to the end. Whether as a humble shepherd boy or an obscure musician before King Saul, from his youth onward he showed himself faithful and trustworthy. Even after his promotion to the highest position in the land, David still modeled integrity and humility. What a man of God!

But, as we shall see, David—like us—was anything but perfect. Having earned the public's trust and respect, he forfeited it all in a brief season of sensual pleasure. Then, as the consequences kicked in, we discover other sides of his makeup—lustfulness as a man, weakness as a father, and partiality as a leader. The aftermath left him beaten down. But through it all, he endured.

It's all there, written for all of us to learn from, preserved for us to remember. This great man, though far from perfect, nevertheless lived a life with strengths worth emulating.

While taking this in-depth journey through the life of David, my hope is that you'll view David as a real person, and then see comparisons and opportunities in your own life so that you begin to emulate the qualities that made him a man after God's own heart.

For a world in desperate need of models worth following, here's someone who well deserves our time and attention: David, a man of valor and grace, of passion and destiny.

CHAPTER 1

GOD'S HEART, GOD'S MAN, GOD'S WAYS

On the surface, there seemed to be nothing about David that would have impressed God, causing Him to say, "That's My man!" David looked much like any other Jewish boy his age. The prophet Samuel observed that he was "reddish, with beautiful eyes and a handsome appearance" (1 Samuel 16:12 NASB)—it's the only physical description of young David we have. Attractive eyes, a healthy complexion, and perhaps he had red hair, or more likely he was reddened or bronzed from hours spent in the sun and wind. The outward appearance didn't seem to set him apart in any special way.

He was just a shepherd—a young one at that—living in the village of Bethlehem. Yet God said, in effect, "You have what I'm looking for, young man. You are the future king of Israel."

If we'd been living in the farmhouse next door to David's family in the Judean hills, we might not even have known the name of this youngest son of Jesse. After all, his own father didn't think of including him at an important interview for his offspring, until the interviewer Samuel (on God's royal search errand) asked, "Are these all your sons?"

Jesse tapped his forehead and said, "Oh, almost forgot—there's my youngest. He's out in the field tending sheep."

"Go and fetch him," Samuel said, as we see in 1 Samuel 16.

Suddenly, this young nobody—a boy even his own father had forgotten about—became somebody.

But before we get to David as king of Israel, let's mine some background and history to better appreciate the world in which he lived. One historian described those ancient times perfectly in one sentence: "The people were on a long drift from God."[1] That was the world into which David was born.

The high priest Eli and his wicked sons were gone, and God's chosen successor—Samuel, last of the famous "judges"—was an old man. People had heard stories about the days when Israel was a great nation, and about Samuel at the zenith of his career, subduing Philistines and judging the land wisely and well. But most of them experienced none of that personally.

They knew only that Samuel was an aged man and that he'd appointed his sons to judge Israel. And what a mistake that was! Look at what the Bible says: "His sons, however, did not walk in his ways but turned aside after dishonest gain, and they took bribes and perverted justice" (1 Samuel 8:3 NASB).

People were disillusioned over this, and they wanted something done about it. What they really wanted was a king.

Samuel's advanced age and his wayward sons were not the only reasons behind this desire. The elders of Israel held a summit meeting with Samuel at Ramah—a place in the hill country about five miles north of Jerusalem—and they voiced another reason: "Give us a king to judge us *like all the other nations have*" (8:5 NLT).

People have always wanted to be like everybody else, to do the popular thing—and these folks were no exception. "We're tired of worshiping an invisible God. Everybody says, 'Where's your king?' And we have no answer except 'Oh, He's in the heavens.' We want a real leader here on earth, like other nations have!"

What they did *not* say to Samuel was this: "We want to wait on God to provide the leadership we need."

Their attitude broke Samuel's heart, and he went to God in prayer about it. And God answered: "They are rejecting me, not you. They don't want me to be their king any longer. . . . Do as they ask, but solemnly warn them about the way a king will reign over them" (8:7–9 NLT).

God will let them have exactly what they want. Does He ever!

SAUL, THE PEOPLE'S CHOICE

The man chosen—Saul—is tall, dark, and handsome. That's how people choose kings. They go for someone who looks good. "He'll be a good image for Israel. Saul's our guy." So Saul comes on the scene and sweeps them off their feet. He is forty years old when he starts to rule. He has a measure of humility to begin with, and seems able to rally people around a cause. He has enough moxie to get an army together, and before long the Israelites agree, "He's the man for the job."

But in time he becomes thin-skinned, hot-tempered, and given to seasons of depression, even thoughts of murder. So much for the people's choice!

David is born about ten years after Saul becomes king. He's born into volatile times. The people of Israel are on that long drift from God, and to make matters worse, they're now becoming disillusioned with the leader they've chosen.

What should you do when your king doesn't walk with God—when you've gotten your own way, but everything seems wrong? That's a disillusioning, insecure feeling.

DAVID, THE LORD'S CHOICE

Graciously, God does not abandon His people. Through Samuel, He intervenes.

> And Samuel said to Saul, "You have done foolishly. You have not kept the command of the Lord your God, with which he commanded you. For then the Lord would have established your kingdom over Israel forever. But now your kingdom shall not continue. *The Lord has sought out a man after his own heart*, and the Lord has commanded him to be prince over his people, because you have not kept what the Lord commanded you." (1 Samuel 13:13–14 esv)

The Lord . . . sought out a man . . . Look at that little three-letter word *man*. Only a man—but what a man!

Would it surprise you to learn that more is written about David in the Bible than any other Old Testament character? Abraham has some fourteen chapters dedicated to his life, and so does Joseph. Jacob has eleven. Elijah has ten. The life story of Moses is contained in about forty chapters (plus mention of his name in several other chapters tightly focused on God giving His laws and instructions for worship). But if my count is correct, sixty-six chapters in the Old Testament are dedicated to David, and the New Testament goes on to make fifty-nine references to him.

When you realize how much is said about David in Scripture, coupled with the fact that he's specifically called a man after God's own heart, you can get the feeling that he's some sort of super-phenomenal person. Some superhero. But don't get the wrong idea about why God chose David—or why He chooses anyone, for that matter.

GOD'S WAY OF CHOOSING

To set the record straight, why *does* God choose anyone? Or perhaps the question should be: What kind of people does God choose and use?

To determine that, let's look first at a New Testament passage. In the opening chapters of the apostle Paul's first letter to the believers at Corinth, the context has to do with the way different people viewed the apostle Paul. Jewish readers of Paul's letter would be looking for a miracle, for a sign that proved Paul had authority from God. Meanwhile his non-Jewish Greek readers would be looking only at surface impressions; a person's inner life meant little to the Greeks of that day, who were more influenced by brains, brawn, and beauty.

In light of all this, here's the thrust of Paul's opening message to the Corinthians: "I'm not coming to you with brilliance or human wisdom, and certainly not with any kind of impressionable physique. Instead, I come only in the power of God. And there's a good reason for that."

Note carefully how Paul expressed the reason:

Brothers and sisters, think of what you were when you were called. Not many of you were wise by human standards; not many were influential;

not many were of noble birth. But God chose the foolish things of the world to shame the wise; God chose the weak things of the world to shame the strong. God chose the lowly things of this world and the despised things—and the things that are not—to nullify the things that are, so that no one may boast before him. (1 Corinthians 1:26–29)

I especially like this modern translation of the last part of that passage:

God . . . has chosen the world's insignificant and despised people and nobodies in order to bring to nothing those who amount to something, so that nobody may boast in the presence of God. (1:28–29 MLB)

Paul was telling them, "Look around, Corinthians. You won't find many impressive people in your church." What was the divine reason for that? *So that no one can boast before God.*

That's a principle we tend to forget because many of us are still a lot like the Greeks. When we look for role models, heroes, we're often swayed or impressed by things that are cause for boasting. We want the beautiful people, the brilliant people, the successful people. But God says, "That's not the way I make my choices. I choose nobodies, and I turn them into somebodies." That, in a nutshell, is the story of the life of David.

DAVID'S SERVANT-LEADER QUALITIES

When God scans the earth for potential leaders, He's not searching for angels in the flesh. He's certainly not looking for perfect people (since there are none). He's searching for men and women like you and me, mere people made up of flesh. But He's looking for certain qualities in those people—the same qualities He found in David.

The first quality God saw in David was *spirituality*. He sought out a man *after His own heart*. What does that mean? It means that you're a person whose life is in harmony with the Lord. What's important to Him is important to you. What burdens Him burdens you. When He says, "Go to the right," you go right. When He says, "Stop that in your life," you stop. When He says, "This is wrong and I want you to change," you come to terms with it. That's bottom-line biblical Christianity. You have a heart that's sensitive to the things of God.

This is further confirmed in this often-quoted verse: "For the eyes of the LORD roam throughout the earth, so that He may strongly support those whose heart is *completely* His" (2 Chronicles 16:9 NASB). God looks for men and women whose hearts are totally and absolutely *His*. No locked closets, nothing swept under the rug. When you do wrong, you admit it and immediately come to terms with it. You grieve over sin. You're concerned about those things that displease Him. You long to please God in your actions. You care about the motivations behind your actions. That's true spirituality—and it's David's foremost quality.

Another quality God saw in David was *humility*.

God had already made His choice for Israel's next king when He sent Samuel to find and anoint him. God told his prophet, "I will send you to Jesse the Bethlehemite, because *I have chosen a king for Myself* among his sons" (1 Samuel 16:1 NASB). The Lord had been on a secret surveillance mission in that home in Bethlehem—where He spotted Jesse's youngest son and said in effect, "That's My man!" Jesse didn't know God was there. None of his sons knew. Nobody knew. But God was there and made His choice.

Why David? Because the Lord saw the humility of a servant's heart in this boy David who was faithfully keeping his father's sheep. To further confirm this, look at these statements in the Psalms: The Lord "chose His *servant* David and took him from the sheepfolds" (78:70 NASB); the Lord said, "I have found My *servant* David; with My holy oil I have anointed him" (89:20 NASB). God is saying, "I don't care about slick public images. Show Me a person with the character and heart of a servant. I don't require charisma, or an impressive track record. I care about character! Is this person deeply authentic in their spiritual walk—or only faking it? And are they a genuine servant?"

When you have a servant's heart, you're humble. You don't rebel. You respect authority. You serve faithfully and quietly. A servant doesn't care who gets the glory but wants to make sure the job get done. Servants try to make the person they serve more successful.

That's David. God looked at him out in those fields in the hills surrounding Bethlehem, keeping his father's sheep, faithfully doing his father's bidding—and God passed His approval. While David's brothers were off in the army making rank and trying to fight impressive battles, David—with his servant's heart—was all alone tending sheep.

A third quality David had was *integrity*. Look in Psalm 78 at how God's chosen man operated in leadership responsibilities:

> He chose David his servant
> and took him from the sheep pens;
> from tending the sheep he brought him
> to be the shepherd of his people Jacob,
> of Israel his inheritance.
> And David shepherded them with integrity of heart;
> with skillful hands he led them. (78:71–72 NASB)

Circle that word *integrity*. The Hebrew word translated there as "integrity" is *tamam*; listen to some of its synonyms: "complete, whole, innocent, having simplicity of life, wholesome, sound, unimpaired." It's what you are when nobody's looking. It means being bone-deep honest.

We live in a world that keeps insisting, in many ways, "If you just make a good impression, that's all that matters." If that's your philosophy, you'll never be a man or woman of God. You cannot fake it with the Almighty. He's not impressed with externals. He always focuses on inward qualities that take time and discipline to cultivate.

A SERVANT'S TRAINING

Even before the choice of David as king gets revealed, God has been training him for his leadership role. The training ground has been lonely, obscure, monotonous, and real. And right there we see four enlightening disciplines.

First, God has trained David in *solitude* on those lonely hillsides. David needed to learn life's major lessons all alone before he could be trusted with responsibilities and rewards before the public. Solitude has nurturing qualities all its own. If you can't stand being alone, you have unresolved conflicts in your inner life. Solitude has a way of helping us address those. When was the last time you got alone with nature and soaked in it—so alone that the sound of silence seemed deafening? That's where David lived, and where he first learned to "king it." He learned to endure burning rays of summer's sun, and he felt blustery winter winds of rain and cold. For many nights he sat alone under the stars, an aloneness that God used to train young David for the throne.

Second, David grew up in *obscurity*. That's another way God trains His best personnel. Men and women of God, servant-leaders in the making, are first unknown and unseen, unappreciated, and unapplauded. In the relentless demands of obscurity, character is built. Strange as it may seem, those who first accept the silence of obscurity are best qualified to handle the applause of popularity.

Which leads us to another discipline of the training ground—*monotony*. We learn to be faithful in the menial, insignificant, routine, regular, unexciting, uneventful, daily tasks of life. Life without a break, without wine and roses. Just dull, plain l-i-f-e.

And that brings us to the fourth discipline: *reality*. You might have thought that despite the solitude, obscurity, and monotony, David was sitting out on those hilltops in a mystic haze, composing great music, or just relaxing in the pastures alongside the sheep. That's not true.

Look ahead with me to 1 Samuel 17. Here's David, standing by King Saul—as a lumbering giant approaches. Remember Saul, the tall-dark-and-handsome guy? Here he is inside his tent, scared to death, knees knocking, hiding from Goliath. And there's little David nearby, saying, "Hey, let's go whip that giant!"

Saul says, "Who are you?"

"I'm David."

"Where have you been?"

"I've been with my father's sheep."

"You can't fight this Philistine," Saul says. "You're just a kid."

Without hesitation, David responds:

"Your servant was tending his father's sheep [that's *solitude, obscurity, monotony*]. When a lion or a bear came and took a lamb from the flock [that's *reality*!], I went out after it and attacked it, and rescued the sheep from his mouth; and when it rose up against me, I grabbed it by its mane and struck it and killed it. Your servant has killed both the lion and the bear; and this uncircumcised Philistine will be like one of them, since he has taunted the armies of the living God." (1 Samuel 17:34–36 NASB)

Where did David get his courage? He learned it all alone before God. David is a man of reality, a man who remains responsible when nobody's looking. So David is thinking, *As for this guy Goliath—I'm not worried about him.* And we know what happened next!

Goliath is no big deal because David has been facing reality long before he squares off against that giant Philistine.

Somehow we have the idea that "getting alone with God" is idealistic, that it's not the real world. But getting alone with God doesn't mean you sit in a closet and think about infinity. No, it means you get alone and discover how to be more responsible and diligent in every area of your life—whether that means fighting lions or bears, or simply following orders.

LASTING LESSONS

David lived so many centuries ago, but the things we can learn from him are as current as this morning's sunrise. Two in particular stand out to me at this point in our discussion.

1. *It's in the little things and the lonely places that we prove ourselves capable of the big things.* If you want to be a person with a large vision, you must cultivate the habit of doing little things well. That's when God puts iron in your bones! The way you fill out those detailed reports, the way you take care of those daily assignments, the way you complete the simple tasks of home or work or school—all this is a reflection of whether you personally are learning to "king it."

The test of our calling is how carefully we cover the bases when nobody's looking.

2. *When God develops our inner qualities, He's never in a hurry.* A notable preacher once put it this way: "The conversion of a soul is the miracle of a

moment; the manufacture of a saint is the task of a lifetime."[2] When God develops character, He works on it throughout a lifetime. He's never in a hurry.

It's in the schoolroom of solitude and obscurity that we learn to become men and women of God. From the schoolmasters of monotony and reality, we learn to "king it." That's how we become—like David—men and women after God's own heart.

GOING AFTER GOD'S OWN HEART: From David's Psalm 26, make his prayer your own:

> Test me, LORD, and try me,
> examine my heart and my mind;
> for I have always been mindful of your unfailing love
> and have lived in reliance on your faithfulness. (26:2–3)

CHAPTER 2

A NOBODY, NOTICED BY NO ONE

After Saul became king of Israel, his actions and decisions soon revealed that he was a selfish, angry, hateful, mean-spirited man—a real piece of work. Eventually something snapped in his mind, and during the later years of his rule, he lost touch with reality, thus proving himself unqualified for the job.

Not long after Saul began his reign, Samuel caught him in three serious infractions (they're laid out for us in 1 Samuel 13–15). These missteps involved a foolish decision, a rash vow against his own son, and finally open disobedience of God.

When Samuel points his finger at the king, Saul tries at first to rationalize what he's done, then finally admits his guilt. Even then, he qualifies his confession:

> Saul said to Samuel, "I have sinned, for I have violated the command of the LORD and your words, *because I feared the people and listened to their voice.* Now then, please pardon my sin and return with me, that I may worship the LORD." (1 Samuel 15:24–25 NASB)

Saul is obviously concerned most about his image. He doesn't want people to know he's sinned. He's telling Samuel, "Let's just go back and worship somewhere together, like we've always done."

Samuel doesn't buy it for a minute. His reply is a straight-from-the-shoulder jab:

> Samuel said to him, "I will not go back with you. You have rejected the word of the LORD, and the LORD has rejected you as king over Israel!"
>
> As Samuel turned to leave, Saul caught hold of the hem of his robe, and it tore. Samuel said to him, "The LORD has torn the kingdom of Israel from you today and has given it to one of your neighbors—to one better than you. He who is the Glory of Israel does not lie or change his mind; for he is not a human being, that he should change his mind." (15:26–29)

Saul, still the rationalizer, again pleads:

> Saul replied, "I have sinned. But please honor me before the elders of my people and before Israel; come back with me, so that I may worship the LORD your God." (15:30)

Okay, so Samuel has caught him in the act—but Saul has confessed, so why not just move on as if nothing happened?

Samuel, being a man of integrity, sees through the whole thing. Clearly, Saul has failed God. But Samuel agrees not to humiliate the king before the people: "Samuel went back with Saul, and Saul worshiped the LORD" (15:31). They participate together that day in a sacrificial ritual of worship—but it's the very last time. "Until the day Samuel died, he did not go to see Saul again, though Samuel mourned for him" (15:35).

The tragic story of Saul is that he never fully repented of his sin. Saul's greatest concern was how he looked before the people. Even after Samuel gave him a break, Saul took advantage of it and continued in that same vein until the day he took his own life.

But that's jumping ahead a bit. After Saul's failures become so clear, the prophet Samuel panics. He has reached the end of his rope. Saul was made king, but he's no longer qualified. What's to be done? Israel is surrounded by enemies, and they need someone to rule and to guard. But who?

Samuel doesn't know. The people don't know either. But God does.

What Samuel doesn't realize—what we ourselves often don't realize—is that behind the scenes, before He ever flung the stars into space, God has had today in mind, and this very week in mind. In fact, He has *you* in mind. And He knows exactly what He's going to do. God is never at a loss about what to do in our daily situations. He knows perfectly well what's best for us. Our problem is, *we* don't know. And we say to Him, "Lord, if You just reveal Your plan to me, explain it all—then I'll count on You." But that's not faith. Faith is counting on Him when we *don't* know what tomorrow holds.

When a man or a woman of God fails, nothing of God fails. When a man or woman of God changes, nothing of God changes. When someone dies, nothing of God dies. When our lives are altered by the unexpected, nothing of God is altered or unexpected. As He said about His praying people through the prophet Isaiah, "Before they call, I will answer; while they are still speaking, I will listen" (Isaiah 65:24 NASB). Before you even utter a word in prayer, God promises: "I'm already answering, bringing to pass the very thing I've planned from the beginning."

That's the beautiful part of this story. Look at how the Lord reveals Himself to Samuel (in a verse we noticed earlier):

> "How long are you going to mourn for Saul, since I have rejected him from being king over Israel? Fill your horn with oil and go; I will send you to Jesse the Bethlehemite, because I have chosen a king for Myself among his sons." (1 Samuel 16:1 NASB)

This is the first Samuel has heard that God was already zeroed in on a particular person to replace Saul as king. God declares that it's someone He selected "for Myself." God is saying, "The people didn't choose this king; he's *My* man."

Then Samuel panics: "But Samuel said, 'How can I go? If Saul hears about it, he will kill me'" (16:2). Samuel is just plain scared. Where are his eyes? Well, they certainly aren't on the Lord. They're riveted on Saul. From a human viewpoint, of course, Samuel is right to be anxious. King Saul has become murderous. But God is completely aware of that. After all, God will be using Saul to shape David's life in the in-between years, between the sheep and the throne. God knows Saul very well.

By the way, do you have a Saul in your life? Is there somebody who irritates and bothers you? God knows all about it. That person is all part of His plan for you, strange as that may seem.

The Lord doesn't answer Samuel's remark about Saul. Instead, He instructs him about how to proceed in Bethlehem:

> The LORD said, "Take a heifer with you and say, 'I have come to sacrifice to the LORD.' Invite Jesse to the sacrifice, and *I will show you what to do.* You are to anoint for me the one I indicate." (16:2–3)

God is saying, "Follow My lead! I'll be showing you exactly what to do—so go do it."

We often think we have to outwit God (in a sense) in order to get His will accomplished in our lives. But to be obedient, we don't have to be smart or clever or perfectly informed; all we have to do is obey. God knows the full situation for each of us—just as He knew for Samuel, as He was telling him, "Take a heifer, go to Jesse, offer the sacrifice, then look around. I'll show you the man I've chosen for the job." It's that simple.

Meanwhile, behind the scenes, there's David—who knows nothing about what Samuel and God are talking about somewhere on the other side of the country. David is just keeping the sheep. That's his job.

With poetic eloquence, British pastor and evangelist F. B. Meyer expressed what David's typical day would be like:

> With the first glimmer of light the boy was on his way to lead his flock to pasture-lands heavy with dew. As the morning hours sped onwards, many duties would engross his watchful soul—strengthening the weak, healing that which was sick, binding up that which was broken, and seeking that which was lost; or the music of his song may have filled the listening air.[3]

That's David. For him, this is just like any other morning. Little does he know his life will never be the same again—that from this day onward, he's destined for the throne of Israel.

God has some extremely exciting things in mind for His children. They may come our way tomorrow, or next month, or next year, or five years down the road; we don't know when they'll show up. But the beautiful thing about this adventure called *faith* is that we can count on Him never to lead us astray. He knows exactly where He's taking us. Our job is to obey, living in close fellowship with God as we walk our earthly path. In the process of that simple arrangement, God engages us in His eternal plan.

"So Samuel did what the LORD told him" (1 Samuel 16:4 NASB). That's it, Samuel! What a model—that's exactly what *we* have to do.

MAN CHOOSES, GOD CORRECTS

Full of expectation, Samuel goes to Bethlehem, Jesse's hometown.

> The elders of the town trembled when they met him. They asked, "Do you come in peace?" (1 Samuel 16:4)

As evident from the elders' immediate reaction here, there's real fear stretched across the land at this time. So when a prophet comes to town: What is he doing *here*? What's wrong? What's happening?

Samuel calms down the town elders:

> Samuel replied, "Yes, in peace; I have come to sacrifice to the LORD. Consecrate yourselves and come to the sacrifice with me." Then he consecrated Jesse and his sons and invited them to the sacrifice. (16:5)

This ancient act of consecration included perhaps the sacrifice of a lamb or other animal, and some kind of liturgical washing for the human participants, and maybe a period of prayer. There was apparently preparation before the anointing, and Jesse and his sons go through this ritual to prepare themselves for what God will say.

So here they are, gathering together, with no clue of what's going to happen. Even Samuel doesn't know which of Jesse's sons God will choose. Seven of them—the seven oldest—are coming closer, looking at Samuel. And he's looking at them.

When they arrived, Samuel saw Eliab and thought, "Surely the LORD's anointed stands here before the LORD." (16:6)

Hey, this must be the one, Samuel is thinking. Eliab looks like the type you'd normally choose for a king. No doubt he's tall and impressive. Certainly he's a man of battle, because in 1 Samuel 17 we see him with Saul and the troops arrayed against Goliath and the Philistines.

What Samuel doesn't see yet is the character of Eliab. He doesn't recognize what we ourselves will discover in chapter 17—that Eliab can be critical and negative and shows contempt toward his youngest brother.

Samuel here is enamored by the externals, as most of us often are. Exhibit A is not God's man—and neither is exhibit B:

Then Jesse called Abinadab and had him pass in front of Samuel. But Samuel said, "The LORD has not chosen this one either." (16:8)

Abinadab, the second oldest, probably looks as impressive as Eliab. For some reason, Abinadab isn't king material either. Neither is exhibit C:

Jesse then had Shammah pass by, but Samuel said, "Nor has the LORD chosen this one." (16:9)

And on it goes:

Jesse had seven of his sons pass before Samuel, but Samuel said to him, "The LORD has not chosen these." (16:10)

In the midst of this parade of possibles, we find God's principle of choice expressed in His words to Samuel:

"Do not consider his appearance or his height, for I have rejected him. The LORD does not look at the things people look at. People look at the outward appearance, but the LORD looks at the heart." (16:7)

God knows our human tendency is to "look at the outward appearance" [the Hebrew says literally, "look at the face"]. God Himself looks always at the heart. If I could change one thing about my focus or vision, it's this: I'd like to see people not by face but by heart. But only God can fully do that. So we, with our limited focus, have to look to Him to give us that kind of discernment. We just don't have it in ourselves.

That's why God repeatedly tells Samuel no in regard to these seven sons of Jesse. He sees these men as they really are. He sees their hearts. Remember, God has indicated that He's already chosen His man. And back in 1 Samuel 13:14 (as we've seen), God "sought for Himself a man after His own heart" (NASB). He knew exactly who that person was.

It's highly significant to me that Jesse doesn't even have his youngest son—son number eight—in the room as Samuel begins this process. Jesse is making two common mistakes that parents make. First, he doesn't have an equal appreciation for all of his children; Jesse seems to see his youngest as nothing more than the sheep-keeper. And second, he has failed to cultivate mutual respect among his sons.

> So he [Samuel] asked Jesse, "Are these all the sons you have?"
>
> "There is still the youngest," Jesse answered. "He is tending the sheep."
>
> Samuel said, "Send for him; we will not sit down until he arrives." (16:11)

With God's help, Samuel gains the proper perspective. Nothing will hinder his pursuit of the one God has chosen! He's telling Jesse, "Go get that boy! What does it matter what he's doing or how old he is?"

MAN FORGETS, GOD REMEMBERS

Oh, for the ability to see beyond the obvious—beyond anyone's age or size or level of intelligence, and even beyond their track record. To see worth and value down deep inside. That's the kind of vision that Samuel, with God's help, finally demonstrates in this beautiful moment. Remember, David's not there; he doesn't know what's going on back home. He's faithfully tending sheep when suddenly someone comes running across the fields with a shout: "Hey, David! They want you back home!"

Obedient to his father's summons, David—just a teenager—walks into the house, still smelling like sheep.

> He was glowing with health and had a fine appearance and handsome features. Then the LORD said, "Rise and anoint him; this is the one."
>
> So Samuel took the horn of oil and anointed him in the presence of his brothers. (1 Samuel 16:12–13)

David sees this old man, Samuel the prophet, suddenly hobble over and pour oil on David's head. It drips down his hair and onto his neck. The ancient historian Josephus wrote that Samuel at this point whispered in the shepherd boy's ear the symbolic meaning: "You will be the next king."

God's ways are so marvelous, aren't they? At the most surprising moment, the most magnificent things happen.

What does David do next? I'm happy to report that he doesn't go around telling everyone, "I'm God's choice!" or hop onto a chariot and race through Bethlehem's streets yelling, "You're looking at Saul's replacement!" Instead, he will soon have a most unusual assignment.

In 1 Samuel 16, the narrative moves next to a scene where King Saul is depressed. At the urging of his attendants, Saul commands that a musician be brought to make him feel better.

> One of the servants answered, "I have seen a son of Jesse of Bethlehem who knows how to play the lyre. He is a brave man and a warrior. He speaks well and is a fine-looking man. And the LORD is with him." Then Saul sent messengers to Jesse and said, "Send me your son David, *who is with the sheep*." (16:18–19)

Don't miss that last phrase. David is back tending sheep, even after being anointed king.

We see it also in the next chapter, where there's a battle going on in the Valley of Elah between Israel and the Philistines with their giant champion, Goliath. Jesse's three oldest sons are with Saul's army, "but David went back and forth from Saul *to tend his father's flock* at Bethlehem" (17:15 NASB)

What's David doing still tending his father's flock? Well, when you have a heart like David's, you do the job that sets before you, and stay faithful to it. Samuel has anointed him with oil, but David doesn't expect special treatment from others. No, he just goes back to the sheep. And when the king says, "Come and play for me," David obeys.

David is sensitive enough to hear the whisper of God's voice: "You will be the next king." But when the big anointing moment is over, he's not searching for the limelight, but humbly back with his sheep. I think that's one of the reasons God sees him as a man after His own heart. He's approachable, believable, authentic—and consistently faithful in the little things.

GOD SPEAKS, WE RESPOND

Three timeless lessons ring through my head as I look at these significant scenes in David's life.

1. God's solutions are often strange and simple. *So be open to them.*

We try to make God complex and complicated. He isn't. Amid all the complications with Saul and the throne, God simply says to Samuel, "Go where I tell you to go. I've got the answer—a new man. You just follow Me, and I'll show you."

Don't make carrying out God's will complicated. It isn't. Stay open to His strange yet simple solutions.

2. God's promotions are usually sudden and surprising. *So be ready.*

When you least expect it, the moment will come—just like the Son of God's return from heaven. Suddenly and surprisingly, He will split the clouds and be with us. Just when we expect Him least, He'll be there, like a thief in the night. And that's the way God's promotions are. He watches you as you faithfully carry out your tasks, and He says, "I know what I'm doing. I know where you are and how to find you. Just stay ready as you carry out your job."

3. God's selections are always sovereign and sure. *So be sensitive.*

God's sovereignty applies to our choosing a mate as well as losing a mate. It applies to our being moved from one place to another, even though we thought we'd remain there ten more years. It also applies to those whom God appoints to fill the shoes of another. How easy to second-guess God's selections! How necessary, when we're tempted to do that, to remind ourselves that His selections are sovereign and sure.

God is looking at your neighborhood and your city, and He's looking for people to whom He can say, "I want to use you there, because you already proved yourself faithful. You are Mine." Our calling is to be faithful in the demanding tasks set before us, whether that involves our education, our marriage, our occupation, our children, or just the daily grind of life. That's the kind of men and women God wants to use.

If you and I had been living in Israel three thousand years ago, our attention would have been greatly focused upon the man Saul, taking the country by storm. Meanwhile, a "nobody" was keeping the sheep for his father on the Judean hillsides near the hamlet of Bethlehem—a boy named David, noticed by no one except God.

———

GOING AFTER GOD'S OWN HEART: From David's Psalm 131, make his prayer your own:

> My heart is not proud, LORD,
> my eyes are not haughty;
> I do not concern myself with great matters
> or things too wonderful for me.
> But I have calmed and quieted myself. (131:1–2)

CHAPTER 3

MUSIC FOR A TROUBLED HEART

Whatever our individual taste, there's something about music that soothes and ministers to us. And right in the middle of the Bible, we find a whole book of it—150 songs. And God is saying, "Sing these often and learn them well—these are My psalms."

More than half of the book of Psalms was written by David. And some of these psalms may well have been written in the context we'll explore next at this season of David's life—as he feels the threatening presence of a madman named Saul.

After Samuel anoints David with oil—indicating that God has chosen him as the next king of Israel, to succeed Saul—we read this: "And the Spirit of the LORD rushed upon David from that day forward" (1 Samuel 16:13 NASB). In utter contrast to this are the very next verses—where we read disquieting things about Saul:

> Now the Spirit of the LORD left Saul, and an evil spirit from the LORD terrified him. Saul's servants then said to him, "Behold now, an evil spirit from God is terrifying you." (16:14–15 NASB)

It's important that we notice that the Spirit of the Lord *left* Saul *before* an evil spirit came.

Christians read those words about "an evil spirit from the LORD" and they fear this could happen to them today. I've heard evangelists use this as a tool to shock Christians. "If you continue living in disobedience," they'll say, "God will lift His Spirit from you and you won't have His presence within you any longer." Then they'll quote this verse about Saul, or they'll quote from Psalm 51 where David himself said to the Lord, "Do not cast me away from Your presence, and do not take Your Holy Spirit from me" (51:11 NASB). That's a fearful thought—that God could lift His Spirit from us and we'd be lost, having once been saved.

So let's go on record now with a good dose of theology. After Jesus rose from the dead and ascended into heaven, the Holy Spirit came upon His followers on the day of Pentecost (as described in Acts 2 in the New Testament). Before that time, the Spirit of God never permanently rested on any believer, except David and John the Baptizer. Those are the only two. It wasn't uncommon in the Old Testament for the Spirit of God to come for a temporary period of strengthening or insight or whatever was needed in the moment, and then to depart, returning again only as needed—then to depart once again.

However, beginning at Pentecost and continuing through our present era, when the Spirit of God comes into the believing sinner at the time of that person's salvation, He never leaves. He comes and baptizes us into the body of Christ. That happens when we truly believe. We remain sealed by the Spirit from that time on. We're never exhorted to *be* baptized by the Spirit; we *are* baptized into the body of Christ. We're placed in His body by the Spirit, sealed until the day of redemption (Ephesians 4:30), as we depart this life. So the Spirit is there, and He never leaves. The New Testament teaches that our bodies are the temple of the Holy Spirit in which the Spirit of God dwells. He permanently resides within us and will never depart.

So, rest easy, Christian friend.

SAUL'S STRANGE DARKNESS

But Saul's situation was centuries before Pentecost, so we shouldn't be surprised to read that in this moment of severity in his life, the Spirit of God departed from him, creating a vacuum—into which God sent an evil spirit to terrify him.

I don't know why God did this. (No one knows.) What seems probable is that God was disgusted with Saul. It's as if He's telling Saul, "I will punish you for presuming on your office as king, and acting against My will. You haven't taken Me seriously. You will learn to do that, Saul—because I'm jealous for My name."

So the Spirit of God departs from Saul and permits an evil spirit to terrify him. The Hebrew verb here for "terrify" is *baath*, which means "to fall upon, to startle, to overwhelm." A reputable Old Testament commentary says that this evil spirit coming upon Saul "was not merely an inward feeling of depression . . . which grew into melancholy, and occasionally broke out in passing fits of insanity"; rather, it was "a higher evil power which took possession of him, and not only deprived him of his peace of mind, but stirred up the feelings, ideas, imagination, and thoughts of his soul to such an extent that at times it drove him even into madness"; and the Lord afflicted Saul with this spirit "as a punishment."[4]

That was Saul's malady. It's so visible to those around him that even his servants realize Saul's need for help. They make a bold suggestion:

> "Let our lord command his servants here to search for someone who can play the lyre. He will play when the evil spirit from God comes on you, and you will feel better." So Saul said to his attendants, "Find someone who plays well and bring him to me." (1 Samuel 16:16–17)

Archaeological studies indicate that the ancients believed in music's power to soothe passions, heal mental diseases, and even hold in check riots and tumults. It's interesting how God uses music to link David to Saul and the throne. (God never runs out of creative ways to carry out His sovereign plan.)

One of Saul's servants, after hearing of the king's need for a good musician, is thinking, *I know a guy who can do that.*

> One of the servants answered, "I have seen a son of Jesse of Bethlehem who knows how to play the lyre. He is a brave man and a warrior. He speaks well and is a fine-looking man. And the LORD is with him." (16:18)

Not a bad recommendation, is it? This candidate is skilled in music, a person of valor, and a warrior; he controls his tongue and he's handsome—and the Lord is with him.

Saul is willing to try anything:

> Saul sent messengers to Jesse and said, "Send me your son David, who is with the sheep." (16:19)

One important thing this tells me is that you should never discount anything in your past. God can pick it up and use it in the most incredible ways. You never know when something that happened years ago will open a door of opportunity into the future. You may think some skill you learned or used long ago is lost, or that you've wasted all your time doing this or that, but don't believe it. God can draw what may seem to be a most insignificant part of your past and put you in exactly the right place to use that particular gift or skill.

That's what happens to David. He's out on the hillsides with the sheep, capturing moments to pluck away on his harp—yet he's ultimately to be Saul's replacement as king. So God works out a way—music!—to bring together these two. Saul's messenger finds David and says, "The king wishes to see you." It all falls together so incredibly. I never cease to be amazed at how perfectly God weaves His will together, without our help.

After receiving Saul's directive, Jesse releases David and loads him down with gifts for the king:

> So Jesse took a donkey loaded with bread, a skin of wine and a young goat and sent them with his son David to Saul. (16:20)

David now trudges along beside a loaded donkey, with his stringed instrument slung over his shoulder.

REFRESHMENT FROM DAVID

David doesn't know it, but he's entering boot camp on the way to becoming a king. That's the way God's program works.

David never once says to Saul, "I'm gonna take your place, pal." He never pulls rank on Saul. He's never jealous or envious of the king's position. He isn't presumptuous. Although he has been anointed as king, he lets the Lord open all the doors—because David is a man after God's heart.

David goes to Saul for one purpose—to be of help to the king:

David came to Saul and entered his service. Saul liked him very much, and David became one of his armor-bearers. (16:21)

And we start to see *why* Saul likes David so much:

Whenever the spirit from God came on Saul, David would take up his lyre and play. Then relief would come to Saul; he would feel better, and the evil spirit would leave him. (16:23)

Isn't that beautiful? Here's Saul on his cot or pacing his bedchamber, writhing in the torment of his depression, and in the corner sits David playing his harp and perhaps singing one of his psalms. Who knows, maybe they sing together after a while. Maybe David teaches Saul some of his songs. Somehow, through David's presence and his soothing music, Saul begins to warmly appreciate this young man who brings him such relief. Through David's unique ability, deliverance from depression becomes a reality.

And so we read that Saul "sent word to Jesse, saying, 'Allow David to remain in my service, for I am pleased with him'" (16:22).

What a statement! The young shepherd has won the heart of the king. So the king tells the shepherd's father, "Let him stay. He's effective! He's got it together."

David, with his primitive stringed instrument, has walked bravely into that dark place where Saul is living. And his music has the right effect: As David plays, "Saul would feel relieved" (16:23 NASB). Another version says, "It eased Saul" (MLB). The Hebrew word translated "relieved" or "eased" is *ravach*, which means "to be wide, to be spacious, to give space so as to bring relief." The Scottish translator James Moffatt put it this way: "He played for Saul till Saul breathed freely." Somehow David's music unleashes the caged feelings inside this tormented man, soothing the savage beast within. The evil presence departs.

God has His hand on this young man whose music not only lifts the heart of a depressed king overwhelmed by blackness, but who will also someday fill a central part of His written Word.

MUSIC ETERNAL

Long before the human voice was heard on the earth, there was music. Did you realize that? In the book of Job, as God was describing to Job how He laid the foundation of the earth, He told us that "the morning stars sang together" (38:7)—meaning either that stars had voices then, or that the angelic host was singing praises to the Creator. I rather believe it was the latter. What glorious harmony this must have been! And if I understand correctly the scenes we see in the last book of the Bible, when we gather around God's throne in eternity, our best expression will be in song. We'll sing, "Worthy is the Lamb, who was slain" (Revelation 5:12).

Since there was singing before the earth was formed, and there'll be singing after the earth is gone—it stands to reason that there should be lots of singing while we're on the earth, right?

Stop and think: In recent weeks, how often have you really sung out your praise to God, just on your own? How easy it is to forget that singing is such an important part of developing our personal worship of God. My own devotional time with the Lord seems to reach its highest point in those moments when I sing my praise to Him.

The Spirit-filled saint is a song-filled saint. And your melody is broadcast right into heaven—live—where God's antenna is always receptive, and where the soothing strains of your song are always appreciated. Never mind how beautiful (or how pitiful) you may sound to yourself; you're not auditioning for the church choir, you're making melody with your heart to the Lord your God! Sing loud enough to drown out the defeating thoughts that normally clamor for attention. Release yourself from that cage of introspective reluctance. *Sing out!* Sing as David did, alone on the hillside or in service to Saul.

And if you listen closely, you may hear the hosts of heaven answering back for joy.

The longer I continue my walk with the Lord, the more I appreciate music's importance. I think Martin Luther was correct when he wrote, "Next to the Word of God, music deserves the highest praise."ʷᵉⁿ Luther believed that the Reformation was not complete until all of God's saints had two things in their possession: a Bible in their own tongue, and a hymnal. He knew we needed the Book that could lead us to a deeper understanding of our faith, plus a companion volume to help us express with joy and delight the depths of that faith—in melody that flows from our voices in song.

God Himself seems to have also cast His vote in favor of music. In His Bible, the longest of all the sixty-six books is Psalms—the one book dedicated to the hymns of the Hebrews, with so many of them written by David. In the preface to C. H. Spurgeon's masterpiece *The Treasury of David*, this great nineteenth-century English preacher wrote, "The delightful study of the Psalms has yielded me boundless profit and ever-growing pleasure."[5] He referred to the Psalms as "this peerless book."

In the twentieth century, the English preacher G. Campbell Morgan called the Psalms "the book in which the emotions of the human soul find expression," and he observed:

> The Psalms range over the whole gamut of human emotions. . . . They were all written for us in the consciousness of, and in the sense of, the presence of God. . . . In every one of these Psalms—from the first to the last, whatever the particular tone, whether major or minor—the singer is conscious of God. That gives peculiar character to the Book of Psalms.[6]

David himself is greatly responsible for that "particular tone" and that "peculiar character" we sense in the Psalms—of the conscious presence of God.

But then, if you actually prefer shallow, superficial lyrics—I'm afraid you're not going to enjoy the Psalms. The Psalms are for those who've decided that music is an art that requires the discipline of keen thinking, as well as a heart that's right before God. It is music for the mature.

Of course a few psalms are indeed widely popular—Psalms 1, 23, and

100, for example. But for the most part, only the mature spend lengthy times in the Psalms. I've observed in fact that only those who are on their way to spiritual maturity spend hours in the Psalms for times of refreshment, times of recovery, times of dealing with their emotions. Always they come back to the Psalms.

Soft music for a hard heart—that's what David provided for Saul. That's the soul music that Christ the Savior provides, and that's where we all must begin. Christ died for us, and He rose from the dead to give us the desire and the power to live a free, positive, fulfilling life outside the cage of human depression and despair. Jesus is our shepherd, and we're His sheep, needing the music of His voice, longing so deeply for it.

In David's wonderful psalms, we find an abundance of worthy patterns for releasing this longing, as we go on to rejoice and exult in God our Savior.

GOING AFTER GOD'S OWN HEART: From David's Psalm 7, make his prayer your own:

> I will give thanks to the Lord because of his righteousness;
> I will sing the praises of the name of the LORD Most High.
> (7:17)

CHAPTER 4

DAVID AND THE DWARF

The most famous battle in the Old Testament was fought not between two armies but between two individuals. It was the battle between David and Goliath in a place called the Valley of Elah.

As we look at that fearsome duel, it's good to remember something the Lord earlier told Samuel, before the prophet first met David: "The LORD doesn't see things the way you see them. People judge by outward appearance, but the LORD looks at the heart" (1 Samuel 16:7 NLT). We look at the externals, so the opinions we form are usually erroneous.

That statement from God about His looking on the heart applies emphatically to the story of this battle. As a warrior, Goliath has everything that would normally impress and intimidate. David, however, has been given the ability to see as God always sees, and he is neither impressed nor intimidated. Because no matter how big and powerful the giant might be, God is greater, and God is all-powerful.

With that in mind, let's survey the battleground:

Now the Philistines gathered their forces for war and assembled at Sokoh in Judah. . . . Saul and the Israelites assembled and camped in the Valley of Elah and drew up their battle line to meet the Philistines. The Philistines occupied one hill and the Israelites another, with the valley between them. (1 Samuel 17:1–3)

The Valley of Elah was wide—the ancient site was probably about a mile in width, with its lower reaches opening even farther. On the valley's floor was a streambed. Rising up about a half-mile on either side of the streambed were great slopes. Bivouacked on one slope is the army of Israel; on the other, the army of the Philistines. That's the setting.

Now let's consider the major characters in our drama.

GOLIATH, FRONT AND CENTER

First there's Goliath, whose size and appearance are so impressive that the writer describes him in exacting detail. First—his height:

> A champion named Goliath, who was from Gath, came out of the Philistine camp. His height was six cubits and a span. (1 Samuel 17:4)

Goliath is an enormous man, somewhere over nine feet tall by our measure. The NBA would love him! If you add to his height the length of his arms when lifted overhead—you can imagine what an imposing creature he must have been. But it isn't just his size:

> He had a bronze helmet on his head and wore a coat of scale armor of bronze weighing five thousand shekels; on his legs he wore bronze greaves, and a bronze javelin was slung on his back. His spear shaft was like a weaver's rod, and its iron point weighed six hundred shekels. His shield bearer went ahead of him. (17:5–7)

The Philistines garbed themselves for battle with a heavy canvas-like undergarment interlaced with overlapping ringlets of bronze. This coat of scale armor went from shoulder to knee as protection against enemy weapons. Body armor of such material and size weighed between 175 and 200 pounds. That was the armor alone; Goliath also wears a bronze helmet, plus bronze leggings (greaves) to protect his shins. And he carries a bronze javelin or spear, the head of which alone weighed 20 to 25 pounds. He also has a shield carrier who walks before him as double protection. The Hebrew word here for "shield" refers to the largest one used in battle, as tall as a full-grown man, protecting his body from enemy arrows.

Allow your mind to picture such an imposing sight. Imagine how frightening it would be to take on a giant of this size protected by this much armor. Clearly, the odds are stacked against anyone foolish enough to try it. And notice this gigantic warrior's talk:

> Goliath stood and shouted to the ranks of Israel, "Why do you come out and line up for battle? Am I not a Philistine, and are you not the servants of Saul? Choose a man and have him come down to me. If he is able to fight and kill me, we will become your subjects; but if I overcome him and kill him, you will become our subjects and serve us." Then the Philistine said, "This day I defy the armies of Israel! Give me a man and let us fight each other." (17:8–10)

Goliath was proposing a common tactic in ancient Eastern warfare—a representative battle, a one-on-one fight. Goliath would represent the Philistine army, and whoever Israel chose would represent the Israelite army. Whoever won, his whole army won; whoever lost, his whole army lost. "There's no reason for your entire army to get involved in this," Goliath is saying. "Just send me your best fighter—and I'll take him on!"

This isn't something Goliath shouted just once; no, his challenge has been repeated twice a day for over a month: "For forty days the Philistine came forward every morning and evening and took his stand" (17:16). Again and again, he comes out and stands there, flaunting his size and strength, daring someone to fight him.

It's a good picture of any "giant" we encounter today—the giants of fear and worry, for example. They don't come just once; they come morning and evening, day after day, night after night, trying relentlessly to intimidate us. The pressure hammers on our heart, yelling across our own personal valley. Few things are more persistent and intimidating than our fears and our worries, especially when we try facing them in our own strength.

ENTER DAVID

Meanwhile, only about ten or fifteen miles away, up in the Judean hills near the little town of Bethlehem, a teenager named David is keeping his father's sheep. He's still too young to be fighting in the army. At this point, David perhaps knows little about what's happening between the Israelite and Philistine armies. He may never have heard of Goliath. But he knows his three oldest brothers are off fighting in Saul's army.

David's father, however, is concerned about those three eldest sons. Jesse is getting old and is probably unable to make the trip himself through the mountains. So he calls his youngest son to send him on an errand:

> "Take this ephah of roasted grain and these ten loaves of bread for your brothers and hurry to their camp. Take along these ten cheeses to the commander of their unit. See how your brothers are, and bring back some assurance from them." (1 Samuel 17:17–18)

David isn't going there to fight, but to bring his brothers food, to make sure they're okay, and to let them know their dad is concerned about them.

The sun rises that morning just like on any other morning for both David and Goliath. But in fact, that forty-first morning of Goliath's challenge will be the last day of his life—and the first day of David's heroic fame.

David rises "early in the morning," and after leaving his flock of sheep with another shepherd, does exactly what his father has told him to do. Imagine what must be going through David's mind as he comes over the top of the last rise and sees and hears the scene below: "He reached the camp as the army was going out to its battle positions, shouting the war cry" (17:20).

No doubt he stands and stares with his mouth open as he sizes up the situation. It's exciting and frightening all at once for this young man who has spent years out on lonely hillsides with only sheep and other shepherds for company (with the occasional lion or bear). He wants to watch—to see what's going to happen. Any kid would. So he moves in closer.

> David left his things with the keeper of supplies, ran to the battle lines, and asked his brothers how they were. As he was talking with them, Goliath, the Philistine champion from Gath, stepped out from his lines and shouted his usual defiance, and David heard it. (17:22–23)

With that loud cry from Goliath from the opposite hillside, suddenly everyone from Israel's camp is rushing to the rear, pulling back—which unfortunately has been their normal reaction: "Whenever the Israelites saw the man, they all fled from him in great fear" (17:24).

Remember that although this is the forty-first day the Israelites have encountered Goliath, for David it's the first time. David has never seen this giant from Gath or heard his challenge. Suddenly he's standing there alone while everyone around him runs for cover (that's how I picture it). He looks across the battlefield and sees this giant encased in armor, shouting threats and defiance, and cursing the God of Israel. Which makes David livid! He's thinking, *No one talks that way about the God of Israel! So why's everybody running?* David has sufficient spiritual character to see the situation clearly—and he isn't intimidated. What a wise young man!

Look at what he does:

> David asked the men standing near him, "What will be done for the man who kills this Philistine and removes this disgrace from Israel? Who is this uncircumcised Philistine that he should defy the armies of the living God?" (17:26)

Now it so happens that Saul has devised an incentive plan for getting someone among his soldiers to kill the giant—and the soldiers have been talking it up (just talk; no action):

> Now the Israelites had been saying, "Do you see how this man [Goliath] keeps coming out? He comes out to defy Israel. The king will give great wealth to the man who kills him. He will also give him his daughter in marriage and will exempt his family from taxes in Israel." (17:25)

But Saul himself is the one man in Israel's camp most qualified to fight Goliath. Remember, Saul's a big man—he's "head and shoulders taller than anyone else in the land" (1 Samuel 9:2 NLT). More importantly, he's the people's leader, his nation's king. But Saul is a coward, the result of his failure to walk with God. So he works out an enticement to get somebody else in the battle in his place. To Goliath's killer, he promises a bride, great riches, and a perpetual tax-exemption plan. Not bad! But even all this isn't enough to prompt a volunteer to go against fearsome Goliath.

The guys around David start telling him about this incentive plan. Meanwhile, what happens next to David is what I call the "older brother" syndrome. Big brother Eliab hears David's conversation with these men.

> And Eliab's anger burned against David, and he said, "Why is it that you have come down? And with whom have you left those few sheep in the wilderness? I myself know your insolence and the wickedness of your heart; for you have come down in order to see the battle." (17:28 NASB)

Don't forget who Eliab really is. He's Jesse's oldest son—back home, he'd been the first center of attention on that day Samuel entered their house. Samuel looked at Eliab and thought, *That's the king!* But no—God put a hand on His prophet's shoulder and whispered, "That's not the one." A short while later, Eliab was watching when the anointing oil was poured on David's head. The oldest brother saw the youngest chosen to be king—the younger blessed above the older. That would be hard for almost any older brother to handle. It certainly was in this instance.

Eliab remembers, and now he gets in his strokes. He asks David, "What are you doing around here anyway?" (17:28 NLT). He's attacking David's motive: "Look, David, why have you *really* showed up in this camp?" Eliab then asks a second question designed to humiliate David: "Hey, where did you leave those sheep?" He's twisting in the knife. Then he gets downright ugly: "I know your insolence; I know the wickedness of your heart. You came here for the excitement. You just want to see the battle." Isn't it interesting how we can so easily and readily see our own guilt in somebody else's life? Because in this scene, the truly insolent and wicked heart is that of Eliab.

At this point, the average person in David's sandals would roll up his sleeves and punch his brother's lights out, rather than dealing with Goliath. David reacts—"Now what have I done? . . . Can't I even speak?" (17:29). But then he ignores his brother and gets on with the important thing—that giant out there. David "turned away to someone else and brought up the same matter, and the men answered him as before" (17:30).

David knows who to fight and who to leave alone. We need to choose our battles wisely. If you don't watch it, you'll find yourself in battles with fellow members of the family of God—while the real enemy of our souls roams around our territory winning victory after victory.

For David, the scene suddenly changes—from standing before Eliab to standing before King Saul. Saul hears about the questions David is asking and the comments he's making, so Saul summons this youth. Keep in mind that King Saul is the guy who doesn't want to fight, though he won't admit it. David, however, is eager for immediate battle.

> David said to Saul, "Let no one lose heart on account of this Philistine; your servant will go and fight him."
>
> Saul replied, "You are not able to go out against this Philistine and fight him; you are only a young man, and he has been a warrior from his youth." (17:32–33)

King Saul is looking at externals, not the heart. And he hasn't learned that God operates differently. Saul is saying, "Look, kid, you don't have the size for it. Just look at that giant!"

As I picture it, David is blinking and thinking, *The only giant in my life is God. And He's omnipotent! If I'm on His side, I can't lose.*

David then describes to Saul how God proved Himself faithful in the past: "The LORD who rescued me from the paw of the lion and the paw of the bear will rescue me from the hand of this Philistine" (17:37).

So often, when facing our own giants, we forget what we ought to remember, and we remember what we ought to forget. We remember our defeats and forget the victories. Most of us can recite the failures of our lives in vivid detail, while being hard-pressed to name the specific and remarkable victories God has pulled off in our past.

Not so with David! He's saying, "I can fight Goliath because the same God who gave me power over a lion and a bear will empower me over this giant. So let me at him!"

That lets Saul off the hook, so he tells David, "Go, and the LORD be with you" (17:37). Isn't it remarkable how people can use spiritual clichés to cover up their empty lives? They know all the right words to use, all the pious-sounding sayings. Saul sure does.

Then we find Saul saying, "Now wait a minute, David. We have to fix you up for battle." Imagine it. You can't tell me the Bible doesn't have humor, because we read here that "Saul dressed David in his own tunic" (17:38). Here's Saul, a size 52 long, while David's a 36 regular. Plus Saul drags out his heavy armor and puts it on David, then drops his oversize helmet onto his head—*clunk!* He puts his heavy sword in David's hand. But David says, "I can't fight with this stuff. I haven't tested all this myself in battle." David drops Saul's sword and slides out of all the armor (17:38–39).

What works for one person will not necessarily work for someone else. We're always trying to put our armor on someone else or put someone else's armor on ourselves—but that's not the way to do battle. It was a great breakthrough in my own life when I finally discovered I could be me, and God would use me. When I tried to wear another person's armor, I just couldn't operate well. God provides unique techniques for unique people.

So here's David, stripped down to his simple garments, armed with his shepherd's sling and staff—ready for battle.

And now—the crucial moment:

> Then he took his staff in his hand, chose five smooth stones from the stream, put them in the pouch of his shepherd's bag and, with his sling in his hand, approached the Philistine. (17:40)

The beautiful thing about this story is that it's a perfect example of how God operates. He magnifies *His* name when we're weak. We don't have to be eloquent or strong or physically attractive. To be blessed of God, we don't have to be beautiful or brilliant or have all the answers. God honors our faith. All He asks is that we trust Him, that we stand before Him in integrity and faith, and He will win our battle. God is just waiting for us to trust Him so He can empower us to battle our giants.

Remember, Goliath is still a giant, still as imposing as ever. David still has all the odds against him. No one in the Philistine camp—or in the Israelite camp either, most likely—would bet on David to win this encounter. But David doesn't need their backing. He needs God, and none other.

After picking up the stones, the shepherd boy approaches the gigantic Philistine warrior. It makes the giant smile. What a joke!

Meanwhile, the Philistine, with his shield bearer in front of him, kept coming closer to David. He looked David over and saw that he was little more than a boy, glowing with health and handsome, and he despised him. He said to David, "Am I a dog, that you come at me with sticks?" And the Philistine cursed David by his gods. "Come here," he said, "and I'll give your flesh to the birds and the wild animals!" (17:41–44)

Intimidation. That's always our major battle when we face giants. But David stands unintimidated before this massive creature:

David said to the Philistine, "You come against me with sword and spear and javelin, but I come against you in the name of the Lord Almighty, the God of the armies of Israel, whom you have defied. This day the Lord will deliver you into my hands, and I'll strike you down and cut off your head. This very day I will give the carcasses of the Philistine army to the birds and the wild animals, and the whole world will know that there is a God in Israel." (17:45–46)

With invincible confidence in his God, David's further words ring out for all the Philistines (not just Goliath) to hear:

"All those gathered here will know that it is not by sword or spear that the Lord saves; for the battle is the Lord's, and he will give all of you into our hands." (17:47)

Here's what David knows perfectly: *The battle is the Lord's.* There it is. That's the secret of David's life.

When giants intimidate us, we get tongue-tied. Our thoughts get confused. We forget how to pray. We focus on the odds against us. Forgetting that we represent God, we stand there with our knees knocking. I wonder what God must think—when all the while He has promised us, "My power is available. There's no one on this earth greater. *Trust Me.*"

David's focus is not on the giant. Intimidation plays no part in his life. What a man! His eyes are fixed on God, because the battle is the Lord's.

Are you trying to command your own battle? Trying to fight it your way? Trying to outsmart the enemy, outfox him? You can't. But God can. And He's saying to you, "Do it My way and I'll honor you. Do it your way, and you're doomed to fail. The battle is Mine."

EXIT GOLIATH

David lives by a simple principle: *Nothing to prove, nothing to lose.* He doesn't try to impress his brothers, or King Saul, or anybody in the army of Israel. He doesn't even try to impress God. He just runs to meet Goliath.

> As the Philistine moved closer to attack him, David ran quickly toward the battle line to meet him. Reaching into his bag and taking out a stone, he slung it and struck the Philistine on the forehead. The stone sank into his forehead, and he fell facedown on the ground.
>
> So David triumphed over the Philistine with a sling and a stone; without a sword in his hand he struck down the Philistine and killed him. (1 Samuel 17:48–50)

To go against a giant wearing two hundred pounds of armor, all David has is a sling and a stone. It may seem silly, but that's the way God operates.

Then there's a *whoosh* as a single stone flies through the air—and that's all there is to it. Goliath falls like a sack full of rocks. David wins.

Got any more giants?

The Philistines don't wait around after that. Seeing their champion dead, they split the scene.

David has to use Goliath's own sword to cut off the giant's head, but notice what he does with Goliath's weapons afterward: "He put the Philistine's weapons in his own tent" (17:54). He drags that huge spear and that heavy sword into his own tent, to keep as a reminder of what God has done. They rest there like silent trophies.

Out of this battle, the real truth emerges, evident to the troops on both sides of the Valley of Elah: The giant here was David; Goliath was a dwarf.

GIANT LESSONS WORTH REMEMBERING

Where do you keep your memories? Don't quickly pass over the victories. Victories won are extremely significant, so remember them.

God doesn't waste victories. When He pulls something off that only He can do, He tells us, "Now don't forget it." In Old Testament times (as in Joshua 4), God had His people pile up huge stacks of stones as reminders of His various victories on their behalf. Those "stones of remembrance" were to remain for all to see and remember.

Four lessons emerge for me from this significant battle between David and Goliath. Read them slowly and remember them well.

1. *Facing giants is an intimidating experience.* We can look back at David's bravery and victory with perfect hindsight and the safe distance of three thousand years. But humanly speaking, imagine what it must have felt like to face—even with the eyes of faith—the intimidating presence of that giant brute. Yet David knew: "My God is greater."

2. *Doing battle is a lonely experience.* No one else can fight for you. Your Goliath is *your* Goliath. Someone might tell you, "Ah, don't worry about that." But to you, it's a Goliath. And nobody else can battle him for you—no counselor or pastor, not even a parent or friend. It's lonely, but it enables you to grow up. On the lonely battlefield, you learn to trust God.

3. *Trusting God is a stabilizing experience.* David brought down Goliath with the first stone. His aim was true, and he didn't miss the mark. We can't know for sure, but from every indication, David had no jitters when he went into battle. He was stabilized by his trust in God. If you try to tackle the giant in the flesh, you can't do it. You'll lose. But when you've spent sufficient time on your knees, it's remarkable how stable you can be.

4. *Winning victories is a memorable experience.* We're to remember the victories of our past. We're to pass on our lion stories, our bear stories, our own Goliath victories.

What's your intimidating giant today? It may relate to your job, your family, or your school. Maybe it's a person, a lawsuit, unemployment, a disaster—maybe even your own partner in life. Perhaps it's some fear lurking around the corner, sucking your energy and draining your faith. God is telling you now, "All I ask of you is five smooth stones and a sling of faith.

I'll take it from there. You don't have to wear somebody else's armor. Just trust Me. I'll strip you down to nothing but faith, then I'll accomplish a victory where I get the glory. *So trust Me.*"

Perhaps you don't know what's lying across the valley. Maybe you can't get a handle on what that giant is, but you sense it's there, haunting you. That uncertainty alone is a giant. But look at that worry in comparison to the Lord God Himself, and say by faith, "The battle is Yours, Lord. I lean on You. I give You all my weapons, all my skills, and I stand before You, trusting You."

It's God's love for us that causes Him to bring us to the end of our own strength. He sees our need to trust Him, and His love is so great that He won't let us live another day without turning over to Him our fears, our worries, even our confusion—so that nothing becomes more significant to us than our Father.

Never forget it: The battle is the Lord's!

GOING AFTER GOD'S OWN HEART: From David's Psalm 70, make his prayer your own:

> As for me, I am poor and needy;
> come quickly to me, O God.
> You are my help and my deliverer;
> LORD, do not delay. (70:5)

CHAPTER 5

HEADED FOR A LONG DARK VALLEY

God never changes. But people certainly do. We change where we live, we change friends, we change jobs. Our interests change, our health changes. Things change at home too: Children are born, children leave home, loved ones are lost.

And how about the challenges and hardships and struggles we face? Just think of the totally unexpected difficulties you've had to face in the past five years. Aren't you glad God didn't tell you about all those things five years ago? Just think of all the stuff you didn't worry about back then because you never saw it coming!

When was the last time you thanked the Lord for not showing you the future? I'm convinced that one of the best things God does for us is to keep us from knowing what will happen beyond today.

We sort of ricochet from moment to moment, trying to put our whole life together. But we lack the time and wisdom to figure it all out. So we have to take life one day at a time. That's the way our unchanging God dispenses life to us—*daily*—because He knows (as you and I don't) what will work together for lasting good in our lives, day by day.

God is good not to show us tomorrow. And the same was true in ancient times, while His Word was being lived out and recorded.

How gracious of God to give David one day at a time. Many people probably suppose that David, after he killed the giant, took the throne within a matter of days, and became Israel's youngest king. But it doesn't happen that way. As a matter of fact, the aftermath of this giant-killing leads David into one of the deepest, longest, and darkest valleys of his entire life. This young man who has proven himself faithful among the sheep and on the battlefield goes from the highest pinnacle of popularity to the lowest depression of despair. God is good not to tell David all that's coming his way.

God's hand is on David. Ultimately, the Lord will use him as the greatest king in Israel's history. But in order to do that, He has to break him, hone him, sharpen him. He has to crush him. David is about to enter the crucible of pain. Thankfully, he has no idea beforehand how excruciating the pain will be.

SUBMISSION TO SAUL—AND ABUNDANT SUCCESS

Against Goliath, David has just accomplished an incredible thing, a stunningly remarkable achievement. A young man not yet twenty years old—who's never worn a soldier's uniform, never suited up with armor to carry a sword onto the battlefield—has killed a giant over nine feet tall with a single throw of his sling.

As a result, David gains instant popularity. He becomes a national hero, an overnight celebrity. People begin to sing his praises. Very few people could take all that in stride—but David does. He knows how to live with success without being tarnished. It's a rare person who can do that, especially if he's young and has never been in the public spotlight. David was that rare person.

Meanwhile, Saul makes good on his promise to enrich the man who killed Goliath. David becomes a permanent part of the king's court and is also given high rank in the army. After that win over Goliath (and Israel's subsequent rout of the Philistines), King Saul isn't going to let this guy go back to herding sheep.

> And Saul took him that day and did not let him return to his father's house. . . . And David went into battle wherever Saul sent him, and always achieved success. (1 Samuel 18:2,5 NASB)

Here's the champion of champions, the giant slayer, and he obediently goes wherever Saul sends him. He's in loyal submission to his king. As a king in the making (without Saul realizing it), David serves as a sort of incognito intern. And the result? He prospers.

Repeatedly in 1 Samuel 18 we're made aware of David's success:

> Whatever mission Saul sent him on, David was so successful that Saul gave him a high rank in the army. This pleased all the troops, and Saul's officers as well. (18:5)

> In everything he [David] did he had great success, because the LORD was with him. (18:14)

> David met with more success than the rest of Saul's officers, and his name became well known. (18:30)

David simply does what God leads him to do. He submits to authority, and God lifts him high above his peers, in great esteem among the people of Israel. David has never served in the army, let alone been in any official role of leadership. But now he commands troops, and he leads so well that even the king's servants are impressed. Despite his youth and inexperience, David knows how to conduct himself with everyone.

If there's a single statement that best describes David at this time in his life, it's a phrase we see twice in this chapter: "The LORD was with him" (18:12,14 NASB).

Interestingly, the Hebrew word translated in this chapter as "prospered" or "success" and "successful" is based on the verb *sakal*, which has to do with being wise. This word "suggests a process of reasoning through complex situations to a practical conclusion, enabling one to act wisely."[7] In Proverbs 10:19 and 21:11, *sakal* is linked to holding one's tongue as well as paying attention to the wise in order to gain wisdom and knowledge. That's the kind of man David is: He guards his lips and keeps a teachable spirit.

No matter how fast our promotion, or how highly we're praised, we're never to lose our teachability. We never reach a level where we're above criticism, or no longer in need of others' input. And frankly, there are times when our best lessons can be learned from our enemies.

FRIENDSHIP WITH JONATHAN—AND
NEEDED ENCOURAGEMENT

Meanwhile, standing in the shadows as David stands before King Saul is another young man, Jonathan, Saul's son. Apparently these two young men haven't met earlier—but immediately their lives are knit together. God knows that David needs an intimate friend to walk with him through the valley ahead of him.

> After David had finished talking with Saul, Jonathan became one in spirit with David, and he loved him as himself. . . . And Jonathan made a covenant with David because he loved him as himself. (1 Samuel 18:1–3)

Intimate friends are rare. Often in our entire lives we have only one, occasionally two, usually not more than three. There's something about an intimate friend that causes your souls to be knit together. It's what we call a kindred spirit.

Intimate friendship has a number of characteristics that we see exemplified in this story.

First, *an intimate friend is willing to sacrifice.* You don't have to beg a close friend for a favor. This is certainly the case with Jonathan.

> Jonathan took off the robe he was wearing and gave it to David, along with his tunic, and even his sword, his bow and his belt. (18:4)

Jonathan wants to give David something meaningful of his own. Friends do that. They're not stingy with their possessions. Later, when life for David gets far tougher, Jonathan will say to him, "Whatever you want me to do, I'll do for you" (20:4). That's the word of an intimate friend. You can hardly impose on an intimate friend; he doesn't keep score. An intimate friend is there to assist whenever and in whatever way is needed. Unselfishness prevails.

Second, *an intimate friend is a loyal defense before others.* He's not a fair-weather friend. He won't talk against you when you're not around.

Later, when Saul's enmity toward David reaches dangerous levels, we read how Jonathan not only stands up for David but also rebukes his father for a wrong attitude toward him:

> Jonathan spoke well of David to Saul his father and said to him, "Let not the king do wrong to his servant David; he has not wronged you, and what he has done has benefited you greatly. He took his life in his hands when he killed the Philistine. The LORD won a great victory for all Israel, and you saw it and were glad. Why then would you do wrong to an innocent man like David by killing him for no reason?" (19:4–5)

What a friend Jonathan is! No pettiness, no envy, no jealousy. After all, as Saul's son, Jonathan would most likely succeed him as king after Saul. Jonathan himself might have wanted the kind of praise that people are bestowing on this kid from the hills of Bethlehem. But as David's friend, Jonathan stays faithful in David's defense.

Third, *intimate friends give each other complete freedom to be themselves.* When you've got a friend this close—this interwoven to your own soul—you don't have to explain why you do what you do. You just do it. (Later, we'll see this especially when both men realize David must flee from Saul's presence—and thus from Jonathan as well.) When your heart is broken, you can bleed all over a friend, and he'll understand. He won't reproach you and insist that you straighten up.

And finally, *an intimate friend is a constant source of encouragement.* Again we can look ahead in the story to see how this happens with David and Jonathan:

> While David was at Horesh in the Desert of Ziph, he learned that Saul had come out to take his life. And Saul's son Jonathan went to David at Horesh and helped him find strength in God. (23:15–16)

Think of that. A hit man is after David—King Saul himself! Out in this wilderness, Saul and his warriors might be waiting behind any bush or rock or hill, ready to strike David down at any moment. Saul's murderous hatred haunts David's life—and what does the son of this hit man do? He encourages his friend.

That's the kind of friend to have. At this lowest moment of David's life, Jonathan finds him frightened, beleaguered, stumbling through the wilderness—and he brings him encouragement, helping him find strength in God Himself.

OPPOSITION FROM SAUL—AND LASTING DANGER

We've noted David's aptitude for winsome success—Saul's servants liked him, Saul's troops followed him, and people everywhere praised him. Even Saul, when he wasn't in the evil spirit's grip, had come to love and respect David. But jealousy soon gets in the way of this esteem.

> When the men were returning home after David had killed the Philistine, the women came out from all the towns of Israel to meet King Saul with singing and dancing, with joyful songs and with timbrels and lyres. As they danced, they sang: "Saul has slain his thousands, and David his tens of thousands."
>
> Saul was very angry; this refrain displeased him greatly. "They have credited David with tens of thousands," he thought, "but me with only thousands. What more can he get but the kingdom?" And from that time on Saul kept a close eye on David. (18:6–9)

This young man has defended God's name in an unprecedented way, so people are welcoming and honoring him by singing and dancing in the streets. But Saul becomes "very angry." The Hebrew word translated "angry" is vivid; it is *charah*, which means "to burn within." We would say Saul is doing a slow burn.

Keep in mind that David has done nothing to deserve any negative treatment from Saul. David is a *sakal* man. His motives are right, his actions wise, his leadership effective. He is worthy of people's praise. But in Saul's ears, that praise "displeased him greatly"—the Hebrew word here means "inner turmoil." As Saul does a slow burn, his stomach churns.

He becomes paranoid. David must be after his kingdom! *This giant-killer could easily become a king-killer. What can I do?* "And Saul eyed David with suspicion from that day on" (18:9 NASB).

When imagination is fueled by jealously, suspicion takes over. Then fear intensifies:

> Saul was afraid of David, because the LORD was with David but had departed from Saul. . . . When Saul saw how successful he [David] was, he was afraid of him. . . . Saul realized that the LORD was with David. (18:12,15,28)

Saul sees that God is on David's side—while Saul himself doesn't have that kind of power. It's more than Saul can handle. At this point, dangerous things are likely to occur.

The Bible is so practical, isn't it? Jealousy is a deadly sin, and Saul's jealousy and suspicion have him shackled in prison. Because Saul is operating in that tight radius of fear, worry, and paranoia, his great goal in life becomes twisted. Instead of leading Israel on to bigger and better things, he's focused only on making David's life miserable.

As we'll see, Saul's madness will cause him to lose sight of all wholesome and responsible pursuits—while David, the object of his jealousy, will live like a fugitive for years. How gracious of God not to reveal to David beforehand the pain of these tragic years!

THE HARD ADVENTURE

With that, we leave David for now, and glean a few relevant applications for our lives today:

1. *Not knowing the future forces us to take life one day at a time.* That's the sum and substance of the life of faith. As Jesus taught: "Each day has enough trouble of its own" (Matthew 6:34).

2. *Having an intimate friend helps us face whatever comes our way.* If you don't have a friend, ask God to give you one—someone you can relate to and who'll be a source of encouragement and support.

3. *Being positive and wise is the best reaction to an enemy.* When you see your enemy coming, it's easy to want to roll up your mental sleeves and decide which jab you'll throw. But that's not God's way, and it's not best.

Remember how David handled Saul. David just kept prospering—behaving wisely. And as we'll see, when the heat rose to an unbearable level, David fled the scene. He refused to fight back or get even.

If you're rubbing shoulders with a jealous individual—a roommate, a boss, a friend, even a spouse—remember the model of David.

Living for Christ is the most exciting adventure in the world, but it's hard. It boils down to this: Walking in victory is the difference between doing what pleases us and doing what pleases God. Like David, we need to stand fast and do what's right without tiring of it. Plain and simple, that's what pleases God.

And in the final analysis—isn't that why we're left on this earth?

GOING AFTER GOD'S OWN HEART: From David's Psalm 69, make his prayer your own:

> Rescue me from the mire,
> do not let me sink;
> deliver me from those who hate me,
> from the deep waters.
> Do not let the floodwaters engulf me
> or the depths swallow me up
> or the pit close its mouth over me. (69:14–15)

CHAPTER 6

EVERY SUPPORT REMOVED

In his anger and suspicion over the success of young hero David, King Saul can no longer contain himself.

The writer H. G. Wells described a character in one of his many novels with these words: "He was not so much a human being as a civil war."[8] That's a perfect description of Saul. He becomes a living civil war—miserable, possessed of an evil spirit, mentally broken. A suspicious, angry, jealous man. As a result, he strikes out against his most trusted and trustworthy servant, David.

Picture this volatile scene in your mind—imagine the mounting pressure here for David:

> An evil spirit from God came forcefully on Saul. He was prophesying in his house, while David was playing the lyre, as he usually did. Saul had a spear in his hand and he hurled it, saying to himself, "I'll pin David to the wall." But David eluded him twice. (1 Samuel 18:10–11)

Chances are, you've never had anyone threaten your life, let alone hurl a spear in your direction. But here's David, doing what he can to lighten the king's dark spirits, when suddenly—*whoosh*—a sharp-pointed spear flies past his head. Reality sinks in for David: *This guy's out of his mind.*

Yet the next verse tells us that "Saul was afraid of David" (18:12). Isn't that intriguing? The very people who are out to get us are often the ones most afraid of us. That's certainly the case with Saul and David.

Don't forget that David has done nothing wrong. He's been a model of humility, dependability, and integrity. But now everything's backfiring. God is beginning to pull the supports out from under David, one by one. It must be a terrifying experience for this young man, especially since he's done nothing to deserve such treatment.

GOD REMOVES DAVID'S SUPPORTS

David is now an officer in Saul's army, possibly commanding a battalion or division of men. In that leadership role, he goes out to battle the Philistines, and he wins. And Saul again goes berserk:

> Once more war broke out, and David went out and fought the Philistines. He struck them with such force that they fled before him. But an evil spirit from the Lord came on Saul as he was sitting in his house with his spear in his hand. While David was playing the lyre, Saul tried to pin him to the wall with his spear, but David eluded him as Saul drove the spear into the wall.
> That night David made good his escape. (19:8–10)

This is now the second time Saul has attacked David with a spear. Mark those last words: "David made good his escape"—because you'll hear of this happening again and again during this season of David's life. It becomes a pattern, a means of survival.

The first support David loses is his good position. He's been brought into the army; he's proven himself a faithful and heroic soldier. And now it's gone in the flash of a spear. Never again will he serve in Saul's army.

The next support God removes is David's wife. We haven't talked about her yet—so let's go back a bit in the chronology of David's life. Remember that Saul had promised to give his daughter as a wife to the man who slew Goliath. But Saul's motives aren't pure.

Now Saul's daughter Michal was in love with David, and when they told
Saul about it, he was pleased. "I will give her to him," he thought, "so that
she may be a snare to him and so that the hand of the Philistines may be
against him." So Saul said to David, "Now you have a second opportunity
to become my son-in-law." (1 Samuel 18:20–21)

Saul deceitfully uses his daughter as a pawn. He asks that David pay a
dowry for her that requires him to kill a hundred Philistines. Perhaps Saul
secretly hopes David will be killed instead.

David, however, manages to deliver what Saul asks without losing his
life—which makes Saul even more afraid of him, and more desirous of
killing him.

After David flees from Saul, he goes home to his wife—who deceives
her father so that David can escape:

Saul sent men to David's house to watch it and to kill him in the morning. But Michal, David's wife, warned him, "If you don't run for your life
tonight, tomorrow you'll be killed." So Michal let David down through
a window, and he fled and escaped. (19:11–12)

Saul faces his daughter to find out what this is all about:

"Why have you betrayed me like this and let my enemy escape?" Saul
demanded of Michal.

"I had to," Michal replied. "He threatened to kill me if I didn't help
him." (19:17 NLT)

Her lie doesn't help David; it only deepens Saul's anger, forcing David
to flee. In essence, David's wife deliberately separates from him. Never again
will these two live in harmony. Thus, God has removed another support—
David's wife.

David is now running through the hills, trying to find some secure
place to hide. As we might expect, he goes to Samuel, the man who anointed
him with oil as God's chosen successor to Saul. David finds Samuel in a
place called Naioth.

But then someone informs Saul of David's location. Soon David is on the move again. In the process, he ultimately loses Samuel as a support to lean on.

David's emotional stability is slowly eroding. The once calm, confident young warrior is feeling the squeeze. Once more as we might expect, David goes and finds a familiar face. To his closest friend, David vents his anguish:

> David fled from Naioth at Ramah and went to Jonathan and asked, "What have I done? What is my crime? How have I wronged your father, that he is trying to kill me?" (20:1)

Jonathan can hardly believe how dangerously this conflict is escalating between his father and his friend:

> "Never!" Jonathan replied. "You are not going to die! Look, my father doesn't do anything, great or small, without letting me know. Why would he hide this from me? It isn't so!" (20:2)

David holds nothing back:

> But David took an oath and said, "Your father knows very well that I have found favor in your eyes, and he has said to himself, 'Jonathan must not know this or he will be grieved.' Yet as surely as the LORD lives and as you live, there is only a step between me and death." (20:3)

What a statement! Death is dogging his steps. Ever felt like that? A hair's breadth away from death? Many war veterans have. A man in my former congregation described being in a horrendous battle in Italy in World War II, and his hair turned white virtually overnight. Makes you wonder if perhaps David's hair is beginning to gray, even at so young an age.

David, of course, knows the truth: Saul, in his jealous madness, hates David and indeed wants him dead.

The extended narrative of what happens next, as related in 1 Samuel 20, is storytelling at its most dramatic, highlighted by vigorous and emotionally gripping dialogue between these two young men. I urge you to read the full passage directly from Scripture, in 1 Samuel 20.

To briefly summarize, David proposes a scheme that will provoke Saul to reveal to Jonathan his true attitude toward David. Jonathan then devises a way for secretly reporting the results of this experiment to David. As they solidify the plan's details in an isolated field where they've gone alone, there's a poignant exchange that reveals the personal danger Jonathan is feeling, as well as his unswerving commitment to David:

"If my father intends to harm you, may the LORD deal with Jonathan, be it ever so severely, if I do not let you know and send you away in peace. May the LORD be with you. . . . But show me unfailing kindness like the LORD's kindness as long as I live, so that I may not be killed, and do not ever cut off your kindness from my family—not even when the LORD has cut off every one of David's enemies from the face of the earth."

So Jonathan made a covenant with the house of David, saying, "May the LORD call David's enemies to account." And Jonathan had David reaffirm his oath out of love for him, because he loved him as he loved himself. (20:13–17)

David and Jonathan have come to a moment of truth about what this conspiracy will most likely reveal—and require.

They part, and the plan soon accomplishes its intended objective. What it will reveal is heartbreaking for these two.

At a special feast where King Saul presides, Jonathan tries to explain away David's absence. Saul becomes so infuriated that he throws his spear and tries to kill Jonathan on the spot. "Then Jonathan knew that his father intended to kill David" (20:33)—there could be no further doubt.

Jonathan goes out to the field where David hides in waiting. His particular instructions shouted to the boy he's brought along (to collect the spent arrows) are a prearranged signal to give David in his hideout this message: "You must go, because the LORD has sent you away" (20:22). After Jonathan sends home the boy (who's unaware of the plan), the two friends meet once more alone, face to face, before David flees for good.

The scene ends this way:

After the boy had gone, David got up from the south side of the stone and bowed down before Jonathan three times, with his face to the ground. Then they kissed each other and wept together—but David wept the most.

Jonathan said to David, "Go in peace, for we have sworn friendship with each other in the name of the LORD, saying, 'The LORD is witness between you and me, and between your descendants and my descendants forever.'" Then David left, and Jonathan went back to the town. (20:41–42)

What a crushing moment for David! Now he also loses his closest friend, Jonathan.

It's shameful that on the basis of this scene in particular, some have tarnished the beautiful story of David and Jonathan's friendship by trying to claim that it provides a biblical basis for homosexuality. But theirs was a pure and deep relationship that emphatically kept God at the center. It was a wholesome and God-honoring friendship that He used in both their lives—and even in the future lives of their families.

Then comes the final blow: *David loses self-respect*. That's the last support. In fact, losing that is the lowest tide of anyone's life. Upon leaving Jonathan, David briefly takes refuge with a priest, being less than open about his status as fugitive from Saul. And then: "That day David fled from Saul and went to Achish king of Gath" (21:10).

Gath? Could his destination really be the leading city of the Philistines? This had been the home of Goliath himself! And here's David (of all people) at Gath (of all places), asking to see the Philistine king! Without doubt, David is conspicuous—and he's recognized immediately. Achish's servants make this report to their king:

> "Isn't this David, the king of the land? Isn't he the one they sing about in their dances: 'Saul has slain his thousands, and David his tens of thousands'?" (21:11)

David isn't stupid. But you'll hardly believe what he does next. Read the following carefully as you imagine the scene:

> David took these words to heart and was very much afraid of Achish king of Gath. So he pretended to be insane in their presence; and while he was

in their hands he acted like a madman, making marks on the doors of the gate and letting saliva run down his beard. (21:12–13)

That's David, our champion—foaming at the mouth, scratching on the gate, looking like a madman as foam dribbles onto his beard! David has hit rock bottom.

When every last one of your supports is removed, you yourself begin to erode. You think differently, with strange thoughts. You start losing sight of the truth. And you hit bottom.

But again, never let it be said that the Scriptures lack humor. In the midst of all this tragedy, God offers us a touch of comedy:

Achish said to his servants, "Look at the man! He is insane! Why bring him to me? Am I so short of madmen that you have to bring this fellow here to carry on like this in front of me? Must this man come into my house?" (21:14–15)

"Get rid of him," Achish is telling them; he has enough nuts in his court already.

David finds no relief in the enemy's camp, just like everywhere else. He has lost his position, his wife, his wise counselor, his closest friend—and now his self-respect. Not unlike Job, he's being hit with such back-to-back blows, his head must be spinning nonstop.

THREE WARNINGS ABOUT CRUTCHES

There might be centuries between us and David, but this man and his experiences are more relevant than ever in our times. One of our links with David is our all-too-familiar experience of having our supports stripped away. David knew what this meant, and so do we.

As children, we lean on our parents. In school, we lean on our teachers, our peers, even on education itself. As we head toward some ideal or goal, we lean on our hope for the future. When we reach adulthood, we lean on our job or profession, on our mate, on our financial security. We may lean on an older friend who's like a mentor to us. Yet all these things can become crutches, having bad effects in our lives in certain ways. Three ways in particular come to mind.

First, *crutches become substitutes for God.* We forget this truth: "The eternal God is a hiding place, and underneath are the everlasting arms" (Deuteronomy 33:27 NASB). Only God is to be our ultimate strength. In the final analysis, we're to lean only on His everlasting arms.

Through the prophet Isaiah, the Lord said,

> "Do not fear, for I am with you;
> do not be afraid, for I am your God.
> I will strengthen you, I will also help you,
> I will also uphold you with My righteous right hand."
>   (41:10 NASB)

"I'll hold you up," God says. "But as long as you lean on someone else or some other thing, you won't lean on Me. They become substitutes for Me, so that you're not being upheld by My hand."

Second, *crutches keep our focus horizontal.* When you lean on another person or another thing, your focus is sideways, not vertical. You find yourself constantly looking to (and relying on) that other person or that thing—like that secure bank account. Those things keep our focus horizontal. Human crutches can paralyze the walk of faith.

Third, *crutches offer only temporary relief.* We turn to some remedy that will soothe us or comfort us or dull our pain. People take billions of tablets and capsules each year to find a tranquilizing experience in order to endure the storms of life. I'm not against taking medicine or accepting help when it's necessary. But when we fall back on this as a regular habit rather than on the Lord, our problem intensifies.

God doesn't give temporary relief. He offers a permanent solution.

You may be in the process of having every crutch removed from your life. This creates enormous pain and instability when support you've counted on is torn away. For some, it's represented by a broken romance. You may have witnessed the demise of your marriage. Or you've experienced the death of a dream—what you hoped and planned for has gone up in smoke.

In those times, you have a choice. You can look around for something else or someone else to lean on. Or you can lean on God, and God alone.

LESSONS FOR LEANERS

Here are two big lessons on leaning:

1. *There's nothing wrong with leaning—if you lean ultimately and completely on the Lord.* In fact, being human, many times you *have* to lean on others; you can't walk the life of faith alone. That's why you have Christ and His church. You're built to be a leaner. You've got an inner shrine within your heart, and no one can occupy the shrine like He can occupy it. Nothing wrong with leaning—if you're leaning on the Lord.

2. *Being stripped of all substitutes is the most painful experience on earth.* There's nothing more painful than being stripped of your heart's deepest support. So relieve yourselves of any crutches before He has to take them away. Don't make an idol out of your mate or your children, or of your position, or of some possession. Enshrine the Lord in your heart and lean only on Him.

David needs to learn that all-important principle; maybe you do too.

It will be extremely difficult for him; you can expect the same.

GOING AFTER GOD'S OWN HEART: From David's Psalm 9, make his prayer your own:

> The Lord is a refuge for the oppressed,
> a stronghold in times of trouble.
> Those who know your name trust in you,
> for you, Lord, have never forsaken those who seek you.
> (9:9–10)

CHAPTER 7

INTO THE CAVE

David—now feigning insanity before the Philistines in Gath just to survive—has bottomed out. He's lost everything in a downward swirl of events. This man on the run chooses again to slip away: "David left Gath and escaped to the cave of Adullam" (1 Samuel 22:1).

In that cave, David experiences the lowest point of his life to date. To learn what's in his heart and mind at this time, we can read the words of the song (known as a *maskil*) that he will compose about it—Psalm 142, which from ancient times has carried this title: "A *maskil* of David. When he was in the cave. A prayer."

As he enters the cave's darkness alone, David in this moment has no security, no promise to cling to, no hope that anything will ever change. He's away from everything and everybody he loved—except God. In these lyrics, he captures what he's feeling, thinking, doing. Here's the full psalm:

> I cry aloud to the LORD;
> I lift up my voice to the LORD for mercy.
> I pour out before him my complaint;
> before him I tell my trouble.
> When my spirit grows faint within me,
> it is you who watch over my way.
> In the path where I walk
> people have hidden a snare for me.
> Look and see, there is no one at my right hand;
> no one is concerned for me.
> I have no refuge;
> no one cares for my life.

I cry to you, LORD;

I say, "You are my refuge,

my portion in the land of the living."

Listen to my cry,

for I am in desperate need;

rescue me from those who pursue me,

for they are too strong for me.

Set me free from my prison,

that I may praise your name.

Then the righteous will gather about me

because of your goodness to me.

Can you feel the lowness and loneliness of this place—and the honest depths of David's desolation? He has no escape, nothing left—yet in the midst of it all, he doesn't lose sight of God. David cries out to Him for deliverance. Here we see the true heart of the man, that inward place that only God fully sees. We sense the qualities that God observed when He chose and anointed the young shepherd boy from Bethlehem.

THE CHALLENGE: START OVER

David has been brought to the point where God can truly begin to shape him and use him. When the sovereign God brings us to nothing, it's to redirect our lives, not end them. Human perspective says, "I've lost so much, failed so much, ruined so much! Why go on living?" And God says, "Because *I* brought you into this cave. And that means it's time to reroute your life—to start anew!"

That's what He does with David. And look at what God provides first:

David left Gath and escaped to the cave of Adullam. When his brothers and his father's household heard about it, they went down to him there. (1 Samuel 22:1)

Remember, not that long ago David's father and brothers were paying little attention to him. So much has happened since then! And here's David—broken, without support, crushed in spirit. And those same brothers and his father now rush to his side.

I have a feeling that at this dismal point in his life, cave-dweller David may have thought he wanted nobody else around—that he's unworthy of anyone's company. But God knows better. God brings his father and brothers crawling into that cave with him, along with the rest of the household.

And they aren't the only ones! Look at what soon happens:

All those who were in distress or in debt or discontented gathered around him, and he became their commander. About four hundred men were with him. (22:2)

What a group! The Hebrew word for "distress" here, *zuk*, means "under pressure." So here come hundreds of pressured people, and people who can't pay their bills, and people who've been wronged and mistreated. No doubt many of them suffer the consequences of Saul's failed leadership over the nation. Some can stand it no longer.

So David ends up with a cave full of malcontents. Can you imagine it? It's bad enough to be there alone, feeling like a worm; but to have four hundred more worms crawl in there with you—what a mess!

But God is at work here. He's rerouting David's life. These four hundred fellow cave dwellers are looking to this man as their leader. That cave is no longer David's escape hatch. It becomes a place of training for the starting core of an army—one that will later be called "David's mighty men of valor." They're a motley crew now, but they'll become his great warriors, and will ultimately assist him in governing the nation when he takes the throne. David will turn their lives around; he'll build into them order, discipline, character, and direction.

David has been beaten down all the way until there's nowhere to look but up. And when he looks up—God is there, bringing to him this bunch of unknowns, little by little, until finally they prove themselves to be Israel's mightiest men. How stunning! Who would ever guess that the next king of Israel is training his troops in a dark cave where nobody sees or cares? How unusual of God! Yet how carefully He has planned it.

At this turning point in life, David makes the crucial decision not to walk away. He accepts his situation and makes the best of it. Those around him need leadership, so he'll provide it—applying the giftedness God has so richly bestowed upon him.

David will grow and thrive in this rugged Judean wilderness with its mountains, ravines, and more caves (which David will also become acquainted with). In this wilderness, David will command a group of mavericks because God wants him to become a maverick king—unlike any other king Israel will ever see.

Later in Scripture we learn that David's men become acutely able with the sword and with the bow and arrow. Obviously, they're being trained. They learn to get their act together in battle. They develop discipline in their ranks. They may be mavericks here at the start, but they're on the way to becoming skilled hunters and courageous fighters.

MORE TO SING ABOUT

Let's look at two other psalms of David's—57 and 34—that appear connected to this season in his life (like Psalm 142). They reveal more of his heart and character. We don't know in what exact order David wrote these songs. But as I look at his life, I like to think of them in the following sequence, with David in a different posture in each one: In Psalm 142 (which we looked at earlier), David's on his face; in Psalm 57, he's on his knees; and in Psalm 34, he's on his feet.

Psalm 57 bears this title: "Of David. A *miktam*. When he had fled from Saul into the cave." And the song opens this way:

> Have mercy on me, my God, have mercy on me,
> for in you I take refuge.
> I will take refuge in the shadow of your wings
> until the disaster has passed.
> I cry out to God Most High,
> to God, who vindicates me.
> He sends from heaven and saves me,

rebuking those who hotly pursue me—
God sends forth his love and his faithfulness. (57:1–3)

At this point, David is on his knees. He's still down, but he's looking up. He's no longer just looking within.

Then he says,

I am in the midst of lions;
I am forced to dwell among ravenous beasts—
men whose teeth are spears and arrows,
whose tongues are sharp swords. (57:4)

This sounds as though it was written when strangers began to crowd into the cave. If you've ever worked with malcontents, you know that's true. They can be thankless, coarse, thoughtless—so overwhelmed with their own needs that they don't pay attention to anyone else's.

So David says to God,

Be exalted, O God, above the heavens;
let your glory be over all the earth. . . .

My heart, O God, is steadfast,
my heart is steadfast;
I will sing and make music. . . .

Be exalted, O God, above the heavens;
let your glory be over all the earth. (57:5,7,11)

Clearly David's eyes are now on his God, the God he exalts. In Psalm 142 he was saying, "There is no one at my right hand; no one is concerned for me . . . no one cares for my life." Now he's certain of God's grace and care. As he's stretched and pulled beyond his limits, he's saying, "You, O God, meet my needs." He's crying out his declaration of dependence.

Let's look now at Psalm 34, where the title reads: "Of David. When he pretended to be insane before Abimelek [likely a dynasty name for Achish, the Philistine king], who drove him away, and he left."

What a difference we see here! What a change has come over David! David begins,

> I will extol the LORD at all times;
> his praise will always be on my lips. (34:1)

And then I imagine David with his men as they're progressing in their battle training, as he says to them,

> Glorify the LORD with me;
> let us exalt his name together. (34:3)

He's putting their eyes on the Lord. He goes on:

> I sought the LORD, and he answered me;
> he delivered me from all my fears. (34:4)

And to the distressed and wounded ones among this group, he says this:

> Taste and see that the LORD is good;
> blessed is the one who takes refuge in him. (34:8)

And to those in debt:

> Fear the LORD, you his holy people,
> for those who fear him lack nothing. (34:9)

To the discontented he says,

> The lions may grow weak and hungry,
> but those who seek the LORD lack no good thing. (34:10)

Finally he gives a wrap-up lesson to the entire group:

> The righteous person may have many troubles,
> but the LORD delivers him from them all. (34:19)

WHY DAVID CHANGED

Why has such a major change taken place in David's life and attitude? I see three reasons.

First, David hurts enough to admit his need. When you're hurting, you need to declare it to someone, and especially to the Lord.

Second, David is honest enough to cry for help. Today, many of us have lived so long under such a veneer of comfort that we hardly know how to cry for help. But God honors such vulnerability. He did then, and He does now.

And third, David is humble enough to learn from God. How tragic that we can live in one cave after another and never learn from God. But not David! I love the man's utter humility as he turns a cave into a training ground for the future.

As I consider this time in David's life, I can't help but reflect upon Jesus and His coming from the glories of heaven to accept a body of malcontents and sinners like us. Some of us are living in an emotional cave—dark, dismal, disillusioning. Perhaps the hardest part of it is that we often can't share the truth about this with anyone.

The Christian life is never just one silver-lined cloud after another, as we soar ever higher. Sometimes the Christian life includes a deep dark cave. But God isn't about to give up on us. If we're in such a cave, He has a purpose for it, for our good. Even if you feel you're the lowest you've ever been, God makes it a beginning point for new growth.

Sometimes life feels like a lonely desert being swept by a dry and barren wind. Something inside us begins to wilt. At other times it feels more like chilling mist that seeps through our pores, numbing our spirit and fogging the path before us. What is it about discouragement that strips our lives of joy and leaves us feeling vulnerable and exposed?

I don't know all the reasons for this, or even many of the reasons. But I do know *one* of the reasons: We don't have a refuge. We all need harbors to pull into when we feel weather-worn and storm-blasted, but shelters are hard to come by these days. Where do you turn when the bottom drops out of your life, or you face an issue that's embarrassing, maybe even scandalous? To whom do you turn when there's no one to tell your troubles to? Where do you find encouragement?

You need a shelter. A listener. Someone who understands. You need a cave to duck into.

David is just such a man in desperate need—and he turns to the living God, and finds in Him a place to rest and repair. After being cornered, bruised by adversity, and while struggling with discouragement and despair, he writes these words in his journal of woes:

> In you, LORD, I have taken refuge;
> let me never be put to shame;
> deliver me in your righteousness. (Psalm 31:1)

Failing in strength and wounded in spirit, David cries out his need for a refuge—a protective place of safety, security, secrecy. David acknowledges that the Lord—Jehovah God—has become his refuge. In Him this troubled man finds encouragement.

And now a final, all-important question: *Why* do we need a refuge? As I read further through David's Psalm 31, I find at least three answers to that question.

1. *We need a refuge first because we're in distress, and sorrow clings to us.* You know those feelings, don't you? Your eyes get red from weeping. The heavy weight of sorrow presses down. Depression, that serpent of despair, slithers silently through the soul's back door. That's when we need a refuge.

2. *We need a refuge because we're sinful, and guilt accuses us.* There's a lot of pain woven through those words. There's embarrassment and guilt. *It's my fault.* What tough words to choke out! "I'm to blame." Harried and haunted by self-inflicted sorrow, we desperately search for a place to hide.

3. *We need a refuge because we're surrounded by adversaries, and misunderstanding assaults us.* Perhaps the most devastating blows are those dealt by others. Tortured by their whisperings, we feel like a wounded mouse in the paws of a hungry cat. The thought of what people are saying is more than we can bear. Gossip gives the final shove as we strive for survival at the ragged edge of despair.

Discouraged people don't need critics. They hurt enough already. They don't need more guilt or piled-on distress. They need encouragement. In a word, they need a *refuge*, a place to hide and heal. They need a willing, caring, available someone to confide in, a comrade at arms. If you can't find one, why not share David's shelter—the One he called "my rock of refuge, a strong fortress to save me" (Psalm 31:2).

We know Him today by the name *Jesus*. He's still available—even to cave dwellers, to lonely people needing someone to care.

GOING AFTER GOD'S OWN HEART: From David's Psalm 61, make his prayer your own:

> Hear my cry, O God;
> listen to my prayer.
> From the ends of the earth I call to you,
> I call as my heart grows faint;
> lead me to the rock that is higher than I.
> For you have been my refuge,
> a strong tower against the foe. (61:1–3)

CHAPTER 8

PAYBACK TIME?

As we've seen, though Saul is large in stature, he's small in character—so small, in fact, that he can't bear to watch someone very much his junior in age and experience being promoted above him—exceeding him in both bravery and popularity.

Because of Saul's deranged enmity, David is forced to become a fugitive in the wilderness of Judea, where he gives his life to training a band of guerrillas, now numbering six hundred. Meanwhile Saul is working overtime to find and kill David:

> So David and his men, about six hundred in number, . . . kept moving
> from place to place. . . . David stayed in the wilderness strongholds and
> in the hills of the Desert of Ziph. *Day after day Saul searched for him*, but
> God did not give David into his hands. (1 Samuel 23:13–14)

God is preparing David for a new kind of role on the throne of Israel. But all David knows—and will know for *years*—is that King Saul dogs his steps every day, eager to wipe him off the earth. And Saul has an army: "Saul called up all his forces for battle, to go down to Keilah to besiege David and his men" (23:8).

Just when it appears that Saul and his army have David and his band surrounded, Saul gets word that the Philistines have raided the land. So Saul breaks off his pursuit and returns to take care of the Philistine problem. Once more, Saul's evil plans are thwarted.

"And David went up from there and lived in the strongholds of En Gedi" (23:29). The name *En Gedi* means "spring of the goat," and this is a perfect hideout for David. I've been to En Gedi, which hasn't changed much since the days of David. It's an oasis in desert wilderness, high above the Dead Sea. It has fresh-water springs, waterfalls, lush vegetation, and countless caves that pockmark the rocky limestone cliffs. En Gedi is a perfect place to hide. It provides protection and water and a natural lookout spot with a view for miles around, revealing any enemy's approach.

Here David and his men take refuge. In battle, the higher location is superior to the lower, and that's where David is—on the high ground. Here he and his men are safe and secure with a bountiful supply of water.

OPPORTUNITY FOR REVENGE

Then Saul returns in pursuit of the man for whom his heart burns with hatred:

> After Saul returned from pursuing the Philistines, he was told, "David is in the Desert of En Gedi." So Saul took three thousand able young men from all Israel and set out to look for David and his men near the Crags of the Wild Goats.
>
> He came to the sheep pens along the way; a cave was there, and Saul went in to relieve himself. David and his men were far back in the cave. The men said, "This is the day the LORD spoke of when he said to you, 'I will give your enemy into your hands for you to deal with as you wish.'" (24:1–4)

The Bible tells a real story, and this unique episode is living proof. In the midst of Saul's mad rush for vengeance, he must answer the call of nature. So he finds himself crouching in the privacy of a cave—but not just any cave. He tromps right into the mouth of a cave where David and his men are hiding farther back. Talk about being vulnerable! Bad enough for the king to be seen at this moment—but to be in the very presence of the enemy! What humiliation.

Worldly wisdom says that when your enemy's vulnerable, it's time to strike. That's what's David's men tell him. "Here's you're opportunity! Here's God's way of getting you into the position He's promised you." Remember, these men are trained to fight. And here's their enemy at his most vulnerable, right there. "Go get him, David! This is it!"

What does David do? "David crept up unnoticed and cut off a corner of Saul's robe" (24:4). Can you picture the scene? Saul's there on his haunches, taking care of business, gazing out the opening of the cave—and David sneaks up behind. Then—*snip*—ever so silently he cuts off a piece of the king's robe.

But later, instead of gloating or glorying over this, David becomes troubled. We read that he's conscience-stricken. Why? All David did was cut off part of the king's robe—when he could have so easily killed Saul, and yet he didn't. So what's the big deal? Who cares about part of a robe? Who's going to notice if the king's hem isn't level anymore? That's the way we all rationalize when we yield to temptation. *Who cares about this little theft, this tiny lie, this slip of the tongue in gossip or anger or insult, this momentary lust?*

There's no such thing as a small step toward temptation, or toward revenge and retaliation. Even a small step in that direction is a wrong step.

David begins to experience justified guilt—because when you really desire to walk with God, you want to come to terms with every detail. You get bothered by little things. You have to make them right. You can't let yourself get away with it. It's when we get away with it and we tell ourselves, *It doesn't matter*—that's when we're on our way to sliding in neck-deep.

That's why David is bothered by what he's done.

He said to his men, "The LORD forbid that I should do such a thing to my master, the LORD's anointed, or lay my hand on him; for he is the anointed of the LORD." (24:6)

When I was in the Marine Corps years ago, they drilled this into us: "You don't salute the man, you salute the rank." If the major's drunk, you salute him because of the rank—he's a major.

That's what David is saying here. "Saul is the king anointed by God. No matter how unfair he has been to me, I have no business dishonoring him."

David is identifying a righteous principle that he's broken. It's true Saul has been in the wrong against David. But is it David's job to make all that right? *No, that's God's job.* "Vengeance is mine, I will repay, says the Lord" (Romans 12:19 ESV). David puts his confidence in this. And he realizes that even in his tantalizing mockery of Saul, he's been operating in the flesh, rather than trusting in God and His righteousness.

> So David persuaded his men with these words and did not permit them
> to attack Saul. And Saul rose up and left the cave and went on his way.
> (1 Samuel 24:7 ESV)

I love this! David not only does the right thing, but he brings along a whole group with him. He *persuades* them with his words. This Hebrew verb's literal meaning, strange as it seems, is "tear apart, pierce through, rip." He tears them apart with his words. I have a feeling that David's dialogue about this with his men may have been heated:

"Sir, the guy's been trying to kill you—now's the chance to take him down! If that's hard for you—let *us* do it!"

"No, men—even cutting that garment wasn't right. So none of us is going after Saul!"

Back and forth they talk, but David persists for a righteous principle until they're persuaded.

Remember this when you're hanging in the balance on something— maybe you've compromised and gone out on the thin ice of rationalization, and God convicts you: "You have no business doing that. Get back where you belong." Then you tell yourself, *But what will others think?* Well, stand firm with God's standards, and you just might persuade others to do the same. Few things are more infectious than a godly lifestyle. The people you rub shoulders with need this kind of challenge every day—to see clean, honest-to-goodness, nonhypocritical integrity, in authentic obedience to God.

David's son Solomon will later write, "When a person's ways are pleasing to the LORD, He causes even his enemies to make peace with him" (Proverbs 16:7 NASB). That's a whale of a promise!

But pleasing the Lord isn't always easy. You say, "I'm gonna live for God, as of today." And I would answer, "That's good—now get ready for battle, because you're surrounded by people who operate in the flesh. Competitive people. Selfish people who are out for what they want. That's where the battle gets heated."

The whole balance of David's story from here on is the working out of this principle—that when our ways are pleasing to the Lord, He overcomes the resistance we face from our enemies.

CONFRONTATION AFTERWARD

Watch what David does next:

> Then David went out of the cave and called out to Saul, "My lord the king!" When Saul looked behind him, David bowed down and prostrated himself with his face to the ground. (1 Samuel 24:8)

After Saul finishes his business in the cave and goes outside, perhaps he walks down a ravine on the other side. Then David steps out of the cave— he's clutching that piece of the king's robe—and calls out across the chasm. This alerts the king, his sworn enemy—but David bows before him, then confronts him:

> He said to Saul, "Why do you listen when men say, 'David is bent on harming you'?" (24:9)

What he's doing is very important. Wrong has been done against David, and when you've been wronged, you need to declare the truth. You're responsible for declaring the truth to whoever has committed the wrong. You cannot change your enemy, but you can make sure he correctly understands the facts. Our tendency often is to just leave it alone: *It'll all work out.* But David didn't leave it alone. He makes it clear that King Saul has been listening to lies—from people saying, "David wants to hurt you." That's false—and David has proof:

"This day you have seen with your own eyes how the LORD delivered you into my hands in the cave. Some urged me to kill you, but I spared you; I said, 'I will not lay my hand on my lord, because he is the LORD's anointed.'

"See, my father, look at this piece of your robe in my hand! I cut off the corner of your robe but did not kill you. See that there is nothing in my hand to indicate that I am guilty of wrongdoing or rebellion. I have not wronged you, but you are hunting me down to take my life." (24:10–11)

David tells Saul the unvarnished truth. "When you were most vulnerable, I didn't strike." He reveals this to the person to whom it mattered most—not to David's comrades or Saul's friends or the people of Israel, but to Saul himself. David comes to terms with his adversary in this conflict:

"May the LORD judge between you and me. And may the LORD avenge the wrongs you have done to me, but my hand will not touch you." (24:12)

David isn't dangling his righteousness before Saul. David isn't built like that; he's a man of integrity. David is simply letting God be God, the righteous judge to whom all vengeance belongs.

To most of us, the response from Saul is startling in the extreme:

"Is that really you, my son David?" Then he began to cry. And he said to David, "You are a better man than I am, for you have repaid me good for evil. Yes, you have been amazingly kind to me today, for when the LORD put me in a place where you could have killed me, you didn't do it. Who else would let his enemy get away when he had him in his power? May the LORD reward you well for the kindness you have shown me today." (24:16–19 NLT)

Let's pause here for a reality check. This is only one case study. I wish I could promise you that whenever you do what's right, your enemy will always quickly see the error of his ways, then turn and tearfully repent and view you correctly. But I can't make that promise.

If someone has wronged you, you're responsible for telling him the truth, but there's no guarantee you can change his perspective about it.

He may die believing the lie. But deep inside your heart, you'll know the fulfillment of having responding righteously. Your conscience will be clear.

Saul not only tearfully confesses his guilt in contrast to David's innocence, but also recognizes David as the next king: "I know that you will surely be king and that the kingdom of Israel will be established in your hands" (24:20). For Saul, the handwriting is on the wall. "You're the man, David—not me."

Then Saul asks David for a favor. In those days, when a dynasty was overthrown, the new regime would typically exterminate everyone in the old regime. So after acknowledging that David will be the next king, Saul pleads for his family:

> "Now swear to me by the LORD that you will not kill off my descendants
> or wipe out my name from my father's family."
>
> So David gave his oath to Saul. Then Saul returned home, but David
> and his men went up to the stronghold. (24:21–22)

Years later, as we'll see, David will keep this promise to Saul. For now, however, David doesn't rejoin Saul. He and his men instead go back to the stronghold—and they're wise to do so. David knows Saul too well. And before long, we'll see Saul once again turn against David.

Astonishingly, this incident in 1 Samuel 24 is echoed later in a highly similar situation. We read about it in 1 Samuel 26, and this time David is in more direct control of the confrontation. The location is "the hill of Hakilah," where Saul and his army have camped—a fact uncovered by David's spies.

> Then David set out and went to the place where Saul had camped. He
> saw where Saul . . . had lain down. Saul was lying inside the camp, with
> the army encamped around him. (26:5)

David and his leading officer Abishai dare to sneak in closer—near enough to kill Saul, as Abishai eagerly points out:

> So David and Abishai went to the army by night, and there was Saul,

lying asleep inside the camp with his spear stuck in the ground near his head. . . . Abishai said to David, "Today God has delivered your enemy into your hands. Now let me pin him to the ground with one thrust of the spear; I won't strike him twice." (26:7–8)

Even more decisively than he did at En Gedi, David states again why he cannot attack this man. He seems to have given extensive thought to all this, with some expectations for the future:

> But David said to Abishai, "Don't destroy him! Who can lay a hand on the LORD's anointed and be guiltless? As surely as the LORD lives," he said, "the LORD himself will strike him, or his time will come and he will die, or he will go into battle and perish. *But the* LORD *forbid that I should lay a hand on the* LORD's *anointed.*
>
> "Now get the spear and water jug that are near his head, and let's go." (26:9–11)

David carries that spear and water jug across a ravine to a hilltop opposite Saul's camp. He calls out blistering words to Abner, the captain of Saul's army:

> "As the LORD lives, you deserve to die, because you have not guarded your master, the LORD's anointed. And now see where the king's spear is, and the jug of water that was by his head." (26:16 NKJV)

Saul hears this too, and he cries out, "Is that your voice, David my son?" (26:17). In answer, David expresses at length how senseless it is for Saul to pursue him. In conclusion, he asserts his utter harmlessness to Saul: "The king of Israel has come out to look for a flea—as one hunts a partridge in the mountains." (26:20)

We're again startled by Saul's response:

> "I have sinned. Come back, David my son. Because you considered my life precious today, I will not try to harm you again. Surely I have acted like a fool and have been terribly wrong." (26:21)

David simply tells Saul to send one of his young men across the ravine to retrieve the king's spear. David is looking to God for help and acceptance—not to Saul. He tells the king,

> "The LORD rewards everyone for their righteousness and faithfulness. The LORD delivered you into my hands today, but I would not lay a hand on the LORD's anointed. As surely as I valued your life today, so may the LORD value my life and deliver me from all trouble." (26:23–24)

Saul gives what might be merely a polite answer:

> "May you be blessed, David my son; you will do great things and surely triumph."

So David went on his way, and Saul returned home.

Once more these two part ways—for the very last time. They'll never see each other again.

A PRACTICAL APPLICATION

All this brings me to helpful guidelines and principles to remember and live by when one person wrongs another.

1. *Since man is depraved, expect to be mistreated.* The same nature beating in the heart of Saul beats in the heart of every person (yourself included). When anyone is controlled by worldliness and the flesh, they'll likely respond as Saul did. So will you. (*Important:* If you're the person guilty of the mistreatment or the offense come to terms with it. Call it sin, and seek reconciliation and restitution.)

2. *Since mistreatment is inevitable, anticipate feelings of revenge.* I'm not saying go ahead and retaliate. But anticipate the feelings of revenge because you can be sure they'll come. It's in our sinful nature. Handling mistreatment correctly doesn't come naturally. Which is why Jesus's truth is so revolutionary: "In everything, do to others what you would have them do to you" (Matthew 7:12). Rare is the individual who will not think about retaliating.

3. *Since the desire for revenge is predictable, refuse to fight in the flesh.* That's why David comes out on top. His men tell him, "Go get him, David"—and I'm convinced he almost does. He plans to kill Saul. But when he comes near the king, by God's grace he gets cold feet. In the incident recorded in 1 Samuel 24, he only cuts off a piece of the royal robe instead of plunging his blade in Saul's back. And in 1 Samuel 26, he only nabs the king's spear while Saul sleeps.

If you're resentful of the way someone has treated you—if you're holding it against that person, hoping you can retaliate or get back—you need to ask God to free you from that bondage. The secret, plain and simple, is forgiveness. Claim God's power to forgive through Jesus Christ. Begin by asking His forgiveness for yourself, for excusing and cultivating the bitterness within your own heart. Ask Him to expose this in all its ugliness, and to put it to death. Jesus Christ, who went through hell for you, can give you the power you need to overcome the worst kind of mistreatment in your life.

The desire for vengeance or revenge—the craving to get even—is in my opinion one of the most subtle and intense temptations in all of life. It feels so justified! It might have to do with an employer who promised you something and didn't come through. Or a friend who walked away when you needed them most, or who betrayed you. It might be a parent or spouse who failed you. Or maybe a coach or teacher who belittled and embarrassed you.

If you're living today in the backwash of any such mistreatment, just waiting for the moment to get even—let God guide you and help you with His instructions:

> If possible, so far as it depends on you, be at peace with all people. *Never take your own revenge*, beloved, but leave room for the wrath of God, for it is written, "Vengeance is Mine, I will repay," says the Lord. . . . Do not be overcome by evil, but overcome evil with good. (Romans 12:18–21 NASB)

How often are you to get revenge? "Never," God says. Not "usually," or "sometimes," or "occasionally." Not even just once! *"Never* take your own revenge."

Now, we're not talking about national defense here, or standing up for what's right in the public arena. We're talking about a personal offense where harm was done specifically to us, and we didn't like it. It's in the past, but we keep fanning the flame by refusing to forgive.

You may be thinking, *That's no problem for me. I've got a handle on that.* But before this day is out, it can happen: You suffer a personal injury, and something deep inside you demands that you strike back. You'll do it, to your own hurt—unless God takes charge.

Learn from David: When life's most subtle temptation attempts to draw you in, refuse to yield. You'll *never* regret forgiving someone who doesn't deserve it!

GOING AFTER GOD'S OWN HEART: From David's Psalm 25, make his prayer your own:

> Guard my life and rescue me;
> do not let me be put to shame,
> for I take refuge in you.
> May integrity and uprightness protect me,
> because my hope, LORD, is in you. (25:20–21)

CHAPTER 9

INSANELY ANGRY

Anger is one of the most debilitating and paralyzing emotions we wrestle with. One reason for this is that it's so unpredictable—it can be on us almost before we know it. And it wears so many different faces. Sometimes it's just an irritation, or the blurting out of a statement or word we later wish we hadn't said. Occasionally, however, it comes with such force that it results in hostile actions.

Another reason it's debilitating is that it's so public. You cannot hide anger; it's on display, there for everybody to witness and remember.

Anger is a choice that easily becomes a terrible habit. The answer, of course, is self-control—which is one thing to say, and another thing entirely to practice.

One psychologist describes this negative emotion at its worst: "Severe anger is a form of insanity. You are insane whenever you are not in control of your behavior. Therefore, when you are angry and out of control, you are temporarily insane."[9]

You may be surprised to know how accurately that describes the great man whose life we're examining. Yes, David—the remarkable man who models patience for years under the spear of Saul—finally loses control. For a time he's temporarily insane with anger. If not for a certain woman who intervenes, the man would have been guilty of murder.

A LITTLE BACKGROUND

In those days, most people who were working out in the field were shepherds. They kept flocks of sheep and herds of goats owned by the wealthy. In our story, the basic problem is a labor conflict—an employer-employee clash. What happens is that David, the employee, plans to kill his boss.

Saul was still king, and while the official fighting of Israel is done by the army under his command, David and his six hundred guerrilla fighters are behind the scenes in the wilderness of Paran, fighting ruffians (who try to steal livestock and plunder small villages) and protecting local shepherds from these attacks.

According to customs of that day, at the time of sheep-shearing, the owner of the animals would commonly set aside a portion of his profit and give it to those who protected his sheep and shepherds while they were out in the fields. It was a way of showing gratitude.

David and his men have been faithfully watching out for the flocks of a man named Nabal, and word reaches them that he's shearing his sheep. So it's payday. It stands to reason, David thinks, that after the careful protection he and his men have provided, it's only fair that they receive some remuneration.

But Nabal, they will learn, is a stingy man.

When we ourselves first meet him, we read that he's "very wealthy" (1 Samuel 25:2). Actually, the Hebrew word means *heavy*—this guy's loaded. Nabal has a lot of money, a lot of sheep, and a lot of goats—in fact, three thousand sheep and a thousand goats. He's clearly a man of great affluence.

His name—*Nabal* means "fool"—is appropriate. In the Scriptures, a fool is notably defined as someone who says there's no God. Nabal lives his life as though there is no God. Furthermore, we're told that he's "surly and mean in his dealings" (25:3).

His wife, Abigail, is just the opposite. We read that she's "an intelligent and beautiful woman" (25:3). She's lovely within and without. Her decisions, as we'll see, are wise. She is governed not by her emotions but by good logical thinking.

There's natural potential here for conflict between husband and wife, and we'll soon see it surface. Their temperaments are different, their behaviors are different, their attitudes are different, their philosophies are different.

ANGER TRIGGERED

Now that it's sheep-shearing time, David follows custom:

> David sent ten young men; and David said to the young men, "Go up to Carmel and visit Nabal, and greet him in my name; and this is what you shall say: 'Have a long life, peace be to you, and peace be to your house, and peace be to all that you have!'" (25:5–6 NASB)

"Shalom, shalom, shalom!" David sends this gracious greeting. "Shalom, Nabal! May your tribe, and your flocks, and your profits increase. Enjoy the goodness of life!"

Also in line with custom, David instructs his messengers to say this:

> "Now I hear that it is sheep-shearing time. When your shepherds were with us, we did not mistreat them, and the whole time they were at Carmel nothing of theirs was missing. Ask your own servants and they will tell you. Therefore be favorable toward my men, since we come at a festive time. Please give your servants and your son David whatever you can find for them." (25:7–8)

It's interesting that David doesn't go to Nabal himself. Perhaps he doesn't want to intimidate the man. Instead, he sends just ten men, enough to bring back what they hope to receive. Maybe it will be a load of lambs. Maybe also a few shekels for each of David's men. Whatever. They'll gladly receive whatever Nabal finds to give. And whatever it is, they'll deserve it—as we learn from a report that comes to Abigail from her husband's employees. It's about David and his warriors:

> These men were very good to us. They did not mistreat us, and the whole time we were out in the fields near them nothing was missing. Night and

day they were a wall around us the whole time we were herding our sheep near them. (25:15–16)

That's quite a report. Obviously David and his men have been effective in protecting Nabal's shepherds from raids by thieves. They've done their job faithfully, efficiently, quietly.

Unfortunately, their employer, Nabal, couldn't care less.

David's men go to Nabal's place, communicate David's greeting, then wait. The response is nothing like what they expect:

Nabal answered David's servants, "Who is this David? Who is this son of Jesse? Many servants are breaking away from their masters these days. Why should I take my bread and water, and the meat I have slaughtered for my shearers, and give it to men coming from who knows where?" (25:10–11)

Notice Nabal's closefisted focus on "*my* bread and water, and the meat *I* have slaughtered." His mind and heart are all about what's *mine*.

David's ten men return empty-handed: "David's men turned around and went back. When they arrived, they reported every word" (25:12).

Then everything breaks loose. Hold on to your seats! The anger of our hero David explodes into temporary insanity.

David said to his men, "Each of you strap on your sword!" So they did, and David strapped his on as well. About four hundred men went up with David, while two hundred stayed with the supplies. (25:13)

Four hundred men! Enough to handle Nabal, don't you think? And all of them, plus David, wear swords—which nobody does just to have a discussion. We therefore have a pretty good idea what's going through David's mind. But talk about overkill! Four hundred men to squash one tightwad!

David has lost control. He's after murder.

In *The Making of the Man of God*, his insightful book on David's life, Alan Redpath wrote this:

David! David! What is wrong with you? Why, one of the most wonderful things we have learned about you recently is your patience with Saul. You learned to wait upon the Lord, you refused to lift your hand to touch the Lord's anointed, although he had been your enemy for so many years. But now, look at you! Your self-restraint has gone to pieces and a few insulting words from a fool of a man like Nabal has made you see red! David, what's the matter?

"I am justified in doing this," David would reply. "There is no reason why Nabal should treat me as he has. He has repaid all my kindness with insults. I will show him he can't trifle with me. It is one thing to take it from Saul, who is my superior at this point. But this sort of man—this highhanded individual—must be taught a lesson!"[10]

Meanwhile, back at the ranch, put yourself in Abigail's sandals. She gets word from her servants that David's on his way to finish off Nabal—and they tell her why:

One of the servants told Abigail, Nabal's wife, "David sent messengers from the wilderness to give our master his greetings, but he hurled insults at them. . . . Now think it over and see what you can do, because disaster is hanging over our master and his whole household. He is such a wicked man that no one can talk to him." (25:14–17)

Note that the servants come to her, not to her husband. Why? Because Nabal isn't approachable, and Abigail is. That's another indication of her wisdom.

ONE WOMAN'S WISDOM

And how should Abigail respond in this situation? Candidly, this could be her opportunity to get rid of an obnoxious loser of a husband! She could say something spiritual like, "Oh, I better pray about this." As those thundering hoofbeats of David's men sweep down the hill, she might still be praying: "Lord, take him swiftly!" It's her chance! After all, Nabal has set himself up for it; it's time he learned a lesson.

That's the way a carnal and worldly person thinks. But observe what happens instead:

> Abigail acted quickly. She took two hundred loaves of bread, two skins of wine, five dressed sheep, five seahs of roasted grain, a hundred cakes of raisins and two hundred cakes of pressed figs, and loaded them on donkeys. Then she told her servants, "Go on ahead; I'll follow you." But she did not tell her husband Nabal. (25:18–19)

Two hundred loaves of bread, and so much more! Can you believe this woman? And she hasn't even told her husband! Sometimes a wife needs to act in favor of her husband and not say a word to him, and here's a classic case in point. For Abigail to approach her obstinate, foolish husband and tell him what she's doing could easily have been instant suicide. He'd never approve.

So she goes ahead and does it on his behalf. I'm not saying she acts against him in secret. I'm saying she acts without his knowledge, yet *in his favor*. She runs interference for the man, and in doing so (as we'll see), she literally saves his life.

Abigail sees Nabal for what he is. She knows his weaknesses. And in his weakest moment, Abigail does not fight—she protects. How gracious of her, and how wise!

Some of the best counsel a man can get comes from his wife, who knows him better than anyone else on earth. For husbands, the finest kind of constructive help and direction and even exhortation they can get often comes from their wives—who know what to do, and when to do it, and the right intention behind it.

Meanwhile David's anger intensifies with each passing mile. We're let into his mindset:

> "It's been useless—all my watching over this fellow's property in the wilderness so that nothing of his was missing. He has paid me back evil for good. May God deal with David, be it ever so severely, if by morning I leave alive one male of all who belong to him!" (25:21–22)

Now picture this. Angry David and his angry men are coming full-tilt down a hill, and Abigail sees them.

As she came riding her donkey into a mountain ravine, there were David and his men descending toward her, and she met them. . . . When Abigail saw David, she quickly got off her donkey and bowed down before David with her face to the ground. (25:20–23)

Abigail has already thought through what she'll do and say. That's the practical side of wisdom. She knows exactly what approach she'll take when she encounters David. It isn't shoot-from-the-hip. She has a thought-through plan, and three things especially stand out about it: her tact, her faith, even her loyalty.

First, she falls on her face, bowing on the ground before David. Moreover, in the speech she'll give him, she calls herself "your servant" six times—and calls David "my lord" eight times. This woman is a study in tactful wisdom.

Her speech begins:

"Pardon your servant, my lord, and let me speak to you; hear what your servant has to say. Please pay no attention, my lord, to that wicked man Nabal. He is just like his name—his name means Fool, and folly goes with him. And as for me, your servant, I did not see the men my lord sent." (25:24–25)

She knows her husband, doesn't she? Everyone knows what he's like, so why hide it? It's useless to try covering up what he's done. Instead she takes the responsibility upon herself. "I wasn't there to give those men you sent a better response."

She now stands as a mediator between her husband and all these men he's unjustly treated:

"And now, my lord, as surely as the LORD your God lives and as you live, since the LORD has kept you from bloodshed and from avenging yourself with your own hands, may your enemies and all who are intent on harming my lord be like Nabal. And let this gift, which your servant has brought to my lord, be given to the men who follow you.

"Please forgive your servant's presumption. The LORD your God will certainly make a lasting dynasty for my lord, because you fight the LORD's battles, and no wrongdoing will be found in you as long as you live." (25:26–28)

What faith she has! She says, "David, I'm looking to you as the next king. Don't ruin your record with a murder! You're bigger than that, David. You've been wronged, but murder isn't the answer. Please pause your intended actions—instead, take what I've provided for your men."

In loyalty to her future king, she looks to David's royal future, and God's hand upon him:

"Even though someone is pursuing you to take your life, the life of my lord will be bound securely in the bundle of the living by the LORD your God, but the lives of your enemies he will hurl away as from the pocket of a sling. When the LORD has fulfilled for my lord every good thing he promised concerning him and has appointed him ruler over Israel, my lord will not have on his conscience the staggering burden of needless bloodshed or of having avenged himself." (25:29–31)

Again she's helping him avoid the tragedy of future regret. "David, you don't need that."

In closing, she adds this: "When the LORD your God has brought my lord success, remember your servant" (25:31). She's saying, "Remember my loyalty to you when the tide turns in your life. That's all I ask."

Oh, what a speech! What a plea!

When you're faced with critical decisions, sometimes you have to do something creative. There's no better handbook than the Bible to guide you in what to do when those times come.

Nabal's life hangs in the balance. And depending on how short David's fuse is—that's how long Nabal will live. His wife realizes that. She knows it will take a lot of food and a pleading message from her to turn David's heart. And we can be certain that along the way she prays fervently for God to intervene.

Often when we're faced with a crisis, the standard response is essentially to run into a corner and hide. But there's a better way. As long as you have breath in your lungs, you have a purpose for living, a reason to exist. No matter how bad your track record might be—marked by disobedience and compromise through most of your life—you're still alive, still existing. And God says, "There's a reason for that. And I'm willing to do creative things through you to put you back on your feet. You can lick your wounds, if that's your choice. But there's a better way." His way will take creativity, determination, and constant focus on the Lord. But when He pulls it off, it's marvelous.

That's what Abigail does with this crisis. And here's David's humble response:

> "Praise be to the LORD, the God of Israel, who has sent you today to meet me. May you be blessed for your good judgment and for keeping me from bloodshed this day and from avenging myself with my own hands." (24:32–33)

What a guy! What a teachable spirit! He has a sword ready to be unsheathed—yet he looks at this woman he's never met and listens to her without interrupting—and it changes his entire demeanor. He's willing to change. Is it any wonder God sees in David a man after His own heart?

May God forever keep us flexible and teachable. When someone has a timely word in regard to any blind spot in our lives—we're fools if we ignore it.

David further models genuine humility here:

> Then David accepted from her hand what she had brought him and said, "Go home in peace. I have heard your words and granted your request." (25:35)

Mission accomplished! Fantastic! Everybody wins. David and his men go back full of food, and all the wiser.

And Abigail goes home—where her husband puts his arm around her and says, "Honey, thanks. You're a great lady! More precious than rubies." No—I *wish* it said that. On the contrary:

> When Abigail went to Nabal, he was in the house holding a banquet like that of a king. He was in high spirits and very drunk. So she told him

nothing at all until daybreak. Then in the morning, when Nabal was sober, his wife told him all these things, and his heart failed him and he became like a stone. (25:36–37)

In loyalty to her husband, she stands between him and death—but the fool is so drunk she can't even tell him about it. So she crawls into bed, pulls up the covers, and goes to sleep. I'm sure she pours out her heart to God and gets things squared away between herself and the Lord, realizing she might never know what it's like to have a husband who appreciates her.

The next morning, she tells hungover Nabal what he missed—that 401 guys had been on their way here to cut off his head. The guy gets really still, and his eyes become glazed—he's having a stroke. Literally. And he'll never recover: "About ten days later, the Lord struck Nabal and he died" (25:38).

Isn't it amazing? When you do what's right, without tiring of it, God takes care of the hardest things imaginable. There's no impossible situation God cannot handle. He might not handle it in the way you envision or think best. But He'll handle it.

Seeing Abigail's faithfulness, God has let her spend the night depending on Him. And shortly thereafter, she buries her husband.

Now listen to David's response:

When David heard that Nabal was dead, he said, "Praise be to the Lord, who has upheld my cause against Nabal for treating me with contempt. He has kept his servant from doing wrong and has brought Nabal's wrongdoing down on his own head." (25:39)

David learns his lesson: If personal vengeance is required—it's always God's responsibility.

For both Abigail and David, this story has a happy ending. After learning of Nabal's death, David sends a marriage proposal to Abigail—and she accepts.

LESSONS FOR FACING CONFLICT

As I think more about this incident in David's life, three things strike me:

1. *Whatever you do when conflicts arise, be wise.* If you're not careful, you'll handle conflicts in the energy of the flesh. Then you'll be sorry.

What do I mean by being wise? I mean look at the whole picture. Resist jumping to quick conclusions and seeing only your side. Look both ways, and weigh the difference. There are always two sides on the streets of conflict.

The other part of being wise is to pray. Get God's perspective. He gives us the wisdom we need when we ask Him for it.

2. *Take each conflict as it comes . . . and handle it separately.* You may have won a battle yesterday, but that doesn't count when today's skirmish comes. You might have great patience today, then lose it tomorrow when the attack comes again. God doesn't give you patience on credit. Every day is a new day to depend on Him.

3. *Whenever you realize there's nothing you can do—wait.* Wait patiently. An impossible impasse calls for a firm application of brakes. Don't keep going. Restrain yourself from anything hasty. Slow down! I've seldom made wise decisions in a hurry. Furthermore, I've seldom felt sorry for things I *didn't* say.

David learned the lesson of patient waiting well, as we learn from his words in Psalm 40:

> I waited patiently for the LORD;
> he turned to me and heard my cry.
> He lifted me out of the slimy pit,
> out of the mud and mire;
> he set my feet on a rock
> and gave me a firm place to stand. (40:1–2)

When you wait patiently for the Lord, your situation may not change— but *you* will. In fact, you may discover that the waiting was all for your benefit, because *you* are what needed to change.

GOING AFTER GOD'S OWN HEART: From David's Psalm 25, make his prayer your own:

> For the sake of your name, LORD,
> forgive my iniquity, though it is great. . . .
> My eyes are ever on the LORD,
> for only he will release my feet from the snare. (25:11–15)

CHAPTER 10

CLOUDY DAYS, DARK NIGHTS

One of the most famous books ever written was penned by a man serving his third term in prison. The man was John Bunyan, and that book—which has influenced the lives of millions of people—is *The Pilgrim's Progress*.

At one point in this story, while Pilgrim is making the long, arduous journey to the Celestial City (representing heaven), he falls into a miry bog called the Slough of Despond. He cannot get out by himself. When he begins to cry out, someone named Help—a picture of the Holy Spirit—reaches down and lifts him out.

If we were to translate Bunyan's Slough of Despond into today's terms, we would call that muddy hole "the pits." There's no way a Christian can go through this life without spending some time in the pits—and that's where we next find David.

There's nothing ethically, morally, or spiritually wrong with experiencing cloudy days and dark nights. They're inevitable. That's why James said, "Consider it all joy . . . *when* you encounter various trials" (James 1:2 NASB).

What does David do after he falls in the mire? That's our concern in this chapter. There's a fork in the road—and he goes the wrong way. The result is misery, compromise, and sixteen long months of disobedience.

David doesn't just happen to tumble into the pits. Looking closer, we see three leading causes.

In the book of 1 Samuel, notice how chapter 27 begins (in various translations): "David thought to himself . . ." (NIV); "David said to himself . . ." (NASB); "David said in his heart . . ." (ESV); "David kept thinking to himself . . ." (NLT). Right there's his first problem. When we talk to ourselves, it's important that we tell ourselves the right thing. David doesn't. This humanistic viewpoint of David's is what leads him first in the direction of the pits. He looks at his situation and sizes it up strictly from the horizontal. You won't find David praying even once in 1 Samuel 27. In fact, David never looks up until much later. During this time he apparently writes no psalms and asks for no help. He simply pushes the panic button repeatedly.

David is coming off a spiritual and emotional high. Though he could have slain Saul, he doesn't. Then he's about to kill Nabal, but Abigail talks him out of it. God has helped him walk in spiritual victory for some time. And as you probably know, coming off the crest of victory can be a very vulnerable spot.

Something else that causes David's descent at this point is his pessimistic reasoning. In that opening verse of 1 Samuel 27, this is what he's telling himself: "One of these days I'll be destroyed by Saul's hand . . ." David should know better. He says, "I *will* be destroyed"—he's talking about the future, but this man doesn't know the future. No one does!

Pessimistic reasoning keeps focusing on the potential downside of the future, and this prompts worry. In the pessimistic mindset, the future is inevitably bleak. So we're not surprised to hear David's prediction: "I will perish" (NASB).

Samuel has anointed him with oil and assured him he will one day be the king. God has spoken to him through Abigail, who reminds him that the Lord appointed him "ruler over Israel" (25:30). God has spoken to him more than once through Jonathan, who has assured his friend, "You'll be the next king." Even his enemy Saul has said, "I know that you will surely be king and that the kingdom of Israel will be established in your hands" (24:20). Yet now David ignores all these promises God has given and convinces himself: "I'll die and never rule Israel. Never!"

Why do we become pessimistic? Because our eyes are on ourselves. The Lord has never led either you or me into a pessimistic thought. Not once. Those thoughts come strictly from within our carnal minds. And they can be devastating.

There's a third reason for David's deep despondency here. It's simply rationalistic logic. Since David has convinced himself of his looming death, he concludes, "The best thing I can do is to escape to the land of the Philistines" (27:1). Surely Saul won't look for him in the enemy's camp!

What a picture this is of a Christian who deliberately opts for carnality. We may not give much thought to the idea of a believer deliberately choosing to disobey God and operate in the flesh. But David at this point is a clear illustration of someone who's a believer on the inside but looks just like a nonbeliever in how he's living.

Psychologist Rollo May wrote, "It is an old and ironic habit of human beings to run faster when we have lost our way."[11] When we lose our way, it's remarkable how quickly we move in the wrong direction and play into the adversary's hand. That's exactly what David does.

You may think this kind of poor decision affects only yourself. I've even heard Christians say, "I'll take my lumps. I'll choose this route and I'll live with the consequences." But nobody takes his lumps alone. You drag others with you. If it's true that no man lives to himself, and no man dies to himself, then we can be certain that no man sins to himself either.

Notice what David's mindset leads him to do:

David and the six hundred men with him left and went over to Achish son of Maok king of Gath. . . . Each man had his family with him, and David had his two wives: Ahinoam of Jezreel and Abigail of Carmel, the widow of Nabal. (27:2–3)

David doesn't retreat alone into Philistine country. David's two wives, Ahinoam and Abigail, go along as well. So do the six hundred men he's trained, his guerrilla troops who are bonded to him. David surely knows these guys will follow him. And these fighting men also bring their households. So now we have David and his family plus six hundred more households.

When you make a decision that's wrong—when you choose a course that isn't God's plan—it affects all those who trust and depend on you, who look up to you and believe in you. Though innocent, they become contaminated by your sinful choices.

And where does David go? He flees again to *Gath*, Goliath's hometown! We've been there before with David. And now he decides he'll live there with Achish the king—archenemy of the Israelites.

THERE ARE CONSEQUENCES

We read: "When Saul was told that David had fled to Gath, he no longer searched for him" (27:4).

An immediate consequence of David's poor decision is that it creates a false sense of security. Saul has stopped following him! So David thinks he's safe now. Nobody's dogging his every move, hunting and haunting him. The pressure's gone! What a relief!

Sin has its temporary pleasures. Disobedience has its exhilarating moments. We're fools if we deny that. There are times when we relax and enjoy disobedience because of those pleasures. But they're passing, short-lived. They *never* bring ultimate satisfaction. Never!

Here's a case in point. Sometimes when we're feeling the intense responsibility of walking with God, we seek a release from that pressure—and we opt for the wrong destination. The relief suddenly comes, and we think, *This is great! It pays off.* When that happens, watch out. Destruction is near.

Another consequence of David's decision is that he submits to his adversary's cause. He calls himself Achish's "servant" (27:5) and asks to be assigned to a place nearby. The Philistine king grants his request and assigns him to the city of Ziklag (27:6).

A third consequence for David is that his compromise continues for a lengthy period: "David lived in Philistine territory a year and four months" (27:7). David ends up staying among the Philistines for sixteen months

Although David is known as "the sweet psalmist of Israel" (2 Samuel

23:1 NASB), not one psalm of his is attributed to these days when he's with Achish in Gath and Ziklag. The sweet singer goes mute. In this spiritual slump, he writes no songs. As the Jewish captives in Babylon would later ask, "How can we sing the songs of the LORD while in a foreign land?" (Psalm 137:4).

In our own compromises we may think, *Oh, it's only for a day or two, then I'll get back into the swing of things.* But it doesn't work like that. There's something magnetic about slumping into despondency and grasping a lost-world lifestyle. The pull is deadly. Scars get formed in our memory, and in the memories of others.

Even Achish will come to see David's decision for what it is: a desertion, a defection. As we'll see, he'll later boastfully defend David's loyalty to himself, when other Philistine leaders have their doubts.

David, who has walked with God, now walks away from Him—into the embracing arms of Israel's enemy. How tragic!

SOWING THE WIND

As David opts for this lifestyle, the winds and storms of entanglement begin to increase in a rapid flow of events.

First of all, a duplicity begins to mark David's steps, a pretentious deception. He pretends to hold one set of feelings while really operating from another entirely.

Deep inside, David is an Israelite. He'll always be an Israelite. But he's trying to make the Philistines think he's on their side. That's what happens when you spend your time in what a pastor friend of mine calls the "carnal corral." There's a conflict of allegiance, with total allegiance lacking on either side. This miserable dilemma creates the need to compromise.

That's precisely what David begins to act out:

Now David and his men went up and raided the Geshurites, the Girzites and the Amalekites. . . . Whenever David attacked an area, he did not leave a man or woman alive, but took sheep and cattle, donkeys and camels, and clothes. Then he returned to Achish. (1 Samuel 27:8–9)

These Geshurites and Girzites and Amalekites are indeed ancient enemies of Israel, and not enemies of the Philistines. Still, they're not Philistine allies either. So David slaughters people who are neither friends nor foes of Philistia.

David is apparently accountable to Achish for his actions, and whenever he returns from raids like these, the king would ask for a report:

> When Achish asked, "Where did you go raiding today?" David would say, "Against the Negev of Judah" or "Against the Negev of Jerahmeel" or "Against the Negev of the Kenites." (27:10)

Duplicity requires vagueness. In David's answer, *Negev* is a broad Hebrew word meaning "south"; David was saying, "Oh, I was fighting down south in Judah"—implying that he was fighting and slaughtering Israelites. But he wasn't. His answers were lies, which is why he wiped out those he fought—so no survivors would be left to report the truth. He was covering his tracks so no Philistines could be certain about what he was up to:

> He did not leave a man or woman alive to be brought to Gath, for he thought, "They might inform on us and say, 'This is what David did.'" And such was his practice as long as he lived in Philistine territory. (27:11)

When you operate in the carnal corral, you need a cloak of secrecy. You don't want to be accountable. You don't want people asking around. So you cover up.

David must have done a good job, because Achish himself believes him:

> Achish trusted David and said to himself, "He has become so obnoxious to his people, the Israelites, that he will be my servant for life." (27:12)

REAPING THE WHIRLWIND

Because David opted earlier for the wrong fork in the road, his resultant lifestyle involves incredible inner turmoil. David will experience injury and devastation. Ultimately, he comes to a point of utter despair.

First, David loses his identity. Achish plans an offensive for his army against the Israelites under Saul, and the Philistines march out "with their units of hundreds and thousands" (29:2), ready to begin the campaign. David and his six hundred fighters are tagging along in the rear with Achish, perhaps serving as the king's protectors.

But Achish begins getting flak from Philistine officers and leaders. They dislike having in their midst David and his men—these Hebrews who've been their sworn enemies in the past. After all, David has in fact killed their mighty champion Goliath.

> The commanders of the Philistines asked, "What about these Hebrews?"
>
> Achish replied, "Is this not David, who was an officer of Saul king of Israel? He has already been with me for over a year, and from the day he left Saul until now, I have found no fault in him." (29:3)

Achish's warm defense of David backfires:

> But the Philistine commanders were angry with Achish and said, "Send the man back, that he may return to the place you assigned him. He must not go with us into battle, or he will turn against us during the fighting. How better could he regain his master's favor than by taking the heads of our own men?" (29:4)

Their guess about what David might do was perhaps right in line with what David is actually contemplating. Regardless, they don't trust David, so Achish has to confront him:

> Achish called David and said to him, "As surely as the LORD lives, you have been reliable, and I would be pleased to have you serve with me in the army. From the day you came to me until today, I have found no fault in you, but the rulers don't approve of you. Now turn back and go in peace; do nothing to displease the Philistine rulers." (29:6–7)

David's show of deep loyalty to Achish—however conflicted it really is—remains on display:

"But what have I done?" asked David. "What have you found against your servant from the day I came to you until now? Why can't I go and fight against the enemies of my lord the king?" (29:8)

When David speaks here of "my lord the king"—perhaps (even subconsciously) he really means the Lord God. But Achish would definitely take these words (just as David wanted him to) as applying only to himself. In response, Achish again warmly praises him, but still insists that David leave—just to make the Philistine leaders happy. "So David and his men got up early in the morning to go back" (29:11). They return to Ziklag, the place Achish had assigned to them.

David is facing a real identity crisis. He has essentially become neither Philistine nor Israelite. Like the carnal Christian, he doesn't feel comfortable in the things of God, but he's now losing interest in his life in the pits. He's like a displaced person. *Who am I? What's my mission? Where am I going? Who has my true allegiance?* Tough questions. No good answers. David is wrestling now with disillusionment. *What did I get myself into?*

Then things get worse, and David (and those with him) will descend into depression:

David and his men reached Ziklag on the third day. Now the Amalekites had raided the Negev and Ziklag. They had attacked Ziklag and burned it, and had taken captive the women and everyone else in it, both young and old. They killed none of them, but carried them off as they went on their way.

When David and his men reached Ziklag, they found it destroyed by fire and their wives and sons and daughters taken captive. So David and his men wept aloud until they had no strength left to weep. (30:1–4)

Imagine yourself in David's position. He and his men crest the hill overlooking the city where he and his men and their families have lived for the past year and a half. But there below they see the entire place burned to the ground—and no living person in sight. Their wives and children have all been taken away as captives by an enemy—by the Amalekites, the same people David raided earlier.

David and his men weep till they have no more tears. If you've cried that long, you know the depth of such depression.

The men's grief turns to anger toward their leader:

David was greatly distressed because the men were talking of stoning him; each one was bitter in spirit because of his sons and daughters. (30:6)

The very people who have looked to David as a guide and friend and leader now turn away. "We don't trust David anymore."

David has reached a point where some people think of taking his life. He's on the bottom rung of the ladder of despair. The last stop. The place where you either jump off into oblivion—or cry out to God for His forgiveness, His help, His rescue.

The wonderful thing is that we always have that choice of crying out to Him—because God never gives up on His children.

David makes the right choice: "David was greatly distressed. . . . But David strengthened himself in the LORD his God" (30:6 ESV). That's it, David! That's the way to handle the Slough of Despond. The pits may seem bottomless, but there's hope above. Reach up! Help is there.

For the first time in sixteen months, David looks up and says, "O God, help me." And God does. He always will. He's a very present help when needed.

Dark days call for right thinking and vertical focus. That's what David learns at this moment in his life. He finds that the Slough of Despond isn't designed to throw him on his back and suck him under; it's designed to bring him to his knees so he'll look up.

Perhaps you've known joys and ecstasies while walking with Christ, but in a moment of despondency you've opted for the wrong fork in the road, and you're now in the camp of carnality. In the words of the prophet, you've been like those who "sow the wind and reap the whirlwind" (Hosea 8:7).

But like David, you've grown tired of feeling displaced. The disillusionment and depression are killing you.

Reach up. Come home. The Father waits at the door—ready to forgive, willing to restore.

It's time to return—to strengthen yourself, yet again, in the Lord your God.

———————

GOING AFTER GOD'S OWN HEART: From David's Psalm 109, make his prayer your own:

> Help me, LORD my God;
> save me according to your unfailing love.
> Let them know that it is your hand,
> that you, LORD, have done it. (109:26–27)

CHAPTER 11

TWO CONTRASTING DEATHS

What do you think those who survive you will write as your epitaph? What will your obituary say? What words will be used in the eulogy to sum up your life? How would you sum it up now, in your own words?

King Saul summed up his own life well in these tragic words spoken to David: "Surely I have acted like a fool and have been terribly wrong" (1 Samuel 26:21).

How aptly that describes the life of Saul. Here was a king who could have been David's role model and mentor—but who instead almost becomes his murderer. Saul started with God on his side—yet he came to live as though God did not exist. There was a great and glorious sunrise in his career when he was anointed as king and affirmed by the people. Outwardly he was a natural leader, winsome as well as strong and physically impressive. He was the man who could do the job. But inwardly, Saul possessed a clear capacity for foolishness—for willful disobedience. In the end, he could only confess about himself, *What a foolish and empty life!*

That life ends tragically. When we read the account, we can hardly believe this is the same Saul who was one day assured by Samuel, "The LORD anointed you ruler over his inheritance. . . . The Spirit of the LORD will come powerfully upon you. . . . Do whatever your hand finds to do, for God is with you" (10:1–8).

The tragic end comes during a Philistine assault against Saul's forces, who occupy a high position on Mount Gilboa:

> The Israelites fled before them, and many fell dead on Mount Gilboa. The Philistines were in hot pursuit of Saul and his sons, and they killed his sons Jonathan, Abinadab and Malki-Shua. The fighting grew fierce around Saul, and when the archers overtook him, they wounded him critically.
>
> Saul said to his armor-bearer, "Draw your sword and run me through, or these uncircumcised fellows will come and run me through and abuse me."
>
> But his armor-bearer was terrified and would not do it; so Saul took his own sword and fell on it. When the armor-bearer saw that Saul was dead, he too fell on his sword and died with him.
>
> So Saul and his three sons and his armor-bearer and all his men died together that same day. (1 Samuel 31:1–6)

As the lost battle becomes a massacre, Saul fears the hated Philistines will torture him, making sport of his dying body. He doesn't want to endure such suffering, or such indignity. In this record of Saul's demise, there's not a word about prayer. How sad that he's so concerned about his image with the enemy while saying nothing about his relationship with God, whom he's about to meet.

That's what happens when disobedience dulls our senses. We stay concerned about what people will do or say, but somehow we've lost contact with what God thinks and what He might do or say.

Saul's death is lacking in glory—and the scene grows worse.

> The next day, when the Philistines came to strip the dead, they found Saul and his three sons fallen on Mount Gilboa. And they cut off his head and stripped off his armor, and they sent messengers throughout the land of the Philistines to proclaim the news in the temple of their idols and among their people. They put his armor in the temple of the Ashtoreths and fastened his body to the wall of Beth Shan. (31:8–10)

It's normal in battle for the victors to strip the enemy dead—to salvage weapons and equipment that might mean their own survival in days to come, if their enemy rallies and the war rages on. But the Philistines do more. After stumbling upon the dead Saul, they mutilate his body, then parade his severed head among their people back home. They hang the rest of his maimed body on a wall to be food for vultures and jackals. Meanwhile Saul's armor is made an offering in the home of pagan idols—where, no doubt, profane comments are cried out about Jehovah, the God of Saul and the Israelites.

Saul—the man who once knew the joys and blessings of God's kingdom, the man chosen as the Lord God's representative to the chosen people, the man who cared so much about his image—is now dead, and his body thoroughly dishonored. The Philistines make jest of the man, make light of his death, and no doubt mock his God.

Saul's defeat destroys Israel's national morale, which only widens the extent of the Philistine victory:

> When the Israelites along the valley and those across the Jordan saw that the Israelite army had fled and that Saul and his sons had died, they abandoned their towns and fled. And the Philistines came and occupied them. (31:7)

What a thoroughly horrible and tragic outcome. And the greatest tragedy of all is that it need never have been. Saul need never have died like this. But the truth of the matter is that he chose this destiny. He chose—inch by inch, day by day—to compromise and to live in disobedience. He was essentially telling God, "I don't need You. I'll live and die as I please." We shouldn't be surprised at the result, but it so clearly could have been avoided. As F. B. Meyer wrote regarding Israel's later captivity,

> This is the bitterest thought of all—to know that one's suffering need not have been; that it has resulted from indiscretion and inconsistency; that it is the harvest of one's own sowing; that the vulture which feeds on the vitals is a nestling of one's own rearing. . . . This is pain![12]

That's what happens when we inch along in compromise or disobedience in our lives, nullifying our testimony, living in mediocrity, choosing the easy way, living like the lost world. So I emphasize again: Saul *chose* a life that led to guilt and despair and bitterness, which need never have been.

It's interesting that Beth Shan—where Saul's mutilated body hangs on a wall—isn't far from where Saul was anointed as king. As Israel's leader, he winds up only a few miles from where he started. Among his countrymen are those who take pity on this man and his dishonored body—the inhabitants of Jabesh Gilead, a town east of the Jordan River:

> When the people of Jabesh Gilead heard what the Philistines had done to Saul, all their valiant men marched through the night to Beth Shan. They took down the bodies of Saul and his sons from the wall of Beth Shan and went to Jabesh, where they burned them. Then they took their bones and buried them under a tamarisk tree at Jabesh, and they fasted seven days. (31:11–13)

A DIFFERENT DEATH

Behind this great tragedy is an interesting analogy between Saul's death and the death of Christ. You might think, *What do Saul and Christ have in common?* I find a number of analogies worth noting.

First, Saul's death appears to be the end of all national hope. Many must have thought, *That's the end of Israel—the Philistines will surely conquer us now.* In a similar way, Christ's death appeared to end all national *and* spiritual hope for those who'd believed in Him. Some of them—observing Jesus on the cross, watching from the safety of the shadows—must have thought, *There's no kingdom of God! We're finished!* Others may have groaned, "Our dream is gone!"

Second, with Saul's death it seems that the adversary has won the final victory. The Philistines march in triumph, displaying Saul's head, no doubt shouting, "We won!" When Christ died, it seemed as though Satan, the adversary of our souls, had won. He must have strutted all over hell declaring, "Victory's mine! I'm the conqueror! *The Messiah is dead.*"

Third, Saul's death ushers in an entirely new plan of operation—David's kingly line, leading to the Messiah. Likewise when Jesus died, a whole new operation was set in motion to fulfill our great salvation.

Fourth, Saul's death opens the opportunity for another to be included in God's line of blessing—namely David. Likewise, Christ's death graciously opened the opportunity of salvation's blessing to the Gentiles, who otherwise would never have been able to come boldly to God's throne of grace.

Fifth, Saul's death ends an era of dissatisfaction and failure, while Christ's death ended an era of law and guilt, introducing an entirely new arrangement based on grace.

Sixth and finally, Saul's death displays foolishness—human foolishness. In human terms, Christ's death displayed the "foolishness" of God—He brings to pass the incredible. Through the preached word, God changes *lives* because of His Son's *death*. They bruised and mocked the body of Jesus, which soon was hurriedly placed in a grave. But God was on the verge of doing the greatest miracle the world has ever known!

If, like Saul, you're living out a need-not-have-been kind of life—it's quite possible the Lord is saying to you, "Now is the time to stop." If so, it's time to answer, "Lord, take over." Ask Him to take control of your life.

DEATH: OUR INESCAPABLE REALITY

Like Saul and his sons, we're all going to die. There's no escaping it. Rather than denying death, we must come to terms with it.

Sometimes death is sudden; sometimes it's long and drawn out. Occasionally it is beautiful, sweet, and peaceful; at other times it's wrenching and hideous, bloody and ugly. There are times when, from our viewpoint, death comes too early. On other occasions, death's cold fingers seem to delay too long, as some dear soul endures pain and sadness, loneliness and senility. But however it comes, there's no escaping it.

Each of us has our own personal appointment with death—unavoidable, unstoppable. But here's the good news for those who know the Lord Jesus Christ: We carry within ourselves a renewed soul and spirit—that part of us which He invaded at the moment we were born from above, when we became Christians. He has taken up His residence there and has given us a new nature. Though our outer being aches and groans and is dying, our inner person is alive and vital, awaiting its home with the Lord. That homecoming occurs the moment we die—yes, that very moment.

> Though our bodies are dying, our spirits are being renewed every day. For our present troubles are small and won't last very long. Yet they produce for us a glory that vastly outweighs them and will last forever! So we don't look at the troubles we can see now; rather, we fix our gaze on things that cannot be seen. For the things we see now will soon be gone, but the things we cannot see will last forever. (2 Corinthians 4:16–18 NLT)

What's most true about your existence today? Is it spiritually alive and authentic? Is it genuinely Christian? Meanwhile, let's return to the questions at this chapter's beginning: What do you think those who survive you will write as your epitaph? What will your obituary say?

———

GOING AFTER GOD'S OWN HEART: From David's Psalm 39, make his prayer your own:

> O LORD, make me know my end
> and what is the measure of my days;
> let me know how fleeting I am!
> Behold, you have made my days a few handbreadths,
> and my lifetime is as nothing before you.
> Surely all mankind stands as a mere breath! . . .
> And now, O Lord, for what do I wait?
> My hope is in you. (39:4–7 ESV)

CHAPTER 12

NEW KING, NEW THRONE, SAME LORD

We've come almost to the halfway point in David's seventy-year life—a good place to stop and take a panoramic view.

A good expression of this wide view is found in the last three verses of Psalm 78. Though brief, they offer a general analysis of the life of David.

> He [the Lord] chose David his servant
> and took him from the sheep pens;
> from tending the sheep he brought him
> to be the shepherd of his people Jacob,
> of Israel his inheritance.
> And David shepherded them with integrity of heart;
> with skillful hands he led them. (78:70–72)

You can find all seventy of David's years wrapped up in these three verses. The Lord chose David as His servant when he was about seventeen. He later took him permanently from the sheep pens after David slayed the giant. Then God installed him as shepherd over His people Israel (or Jacob) at age thirty. Between the years of seventeen and thirty, as we've seen, David was on the run from Saul. Finally at age thirty he comes to that pinnacle moment when he takes the throne of Israel. What happens then? For his final forty years, David shepherds this nation with integrity of heart and guides them with his skillful hands.

David's young adult years were mostly years of triumph, though there were a few temporary excursions in the flesh. But as we'll see, tragedies mount up in the last twenty years of David's life. There's a downhill slide—until, I believe, David dies with a true measure of brokenness.

But there's so much more to a life than just chronology. When we read, "David was thirty years old when he became king, and he reigned forty years" (2 Samuel 5:4), it's easy to forget what led to his being exalted as the king. Our tendency is to focus on the present moment and to forget the yesterdays or the tomorrows. Some of the yesterdays need to be forgotten; some of the tomorrows need to be left to the Lord without worry; we need to keep the perspective on life that God keeps.

Walking down the corridors of our memory is like walking through an art gallery. On the walls are all of yesterday's pictures—our home, our parents, our childhood, our rearing—the heartaches and difficulties, the joys and triumphs, as well as the abuses and inequities of life. Since Jesus Christ our Lord is the same yesterday and today and forever, we can take the Christ of today and walk with Him into our yesterday, and we can ask Him to remove any pictures that bring bad or defeating memories. The Christian can let Jesus invade yesterday and deal with those years of affliction—"The years the locusts have eaten" (Joel 2:25)—and remove those negative scenes that we all have, that bring despair and defeat. And we let Him leave there the murals that bring pleasure and victory.

Because of David's many mighty acts and the legacy he's leaving, it's easy to forget that for a dozen or more years he lived as a fugitive, spending many hours of discouragement and disillusionment in the wilderness. He became a broken, humbled man during those days. He learned much from those crushing years—but little good would come to him later from reliving that pain.

Finally, however, he becomes king—Israel's second king, chosen and anointed by God Himself. How does he take the throne? Does he storm into the role and demand everyone's submission to his rule? No. David is a sensitive man. He has learned through past afflictions (especially as a cave dweller) how to lead and how to rally others around him.

Sometimes we're better at handling affliction than we are at handling success. David at his life's midpoint faces abundant success. His predecessor is dead, having taken his own life. There's room now for David to grip his future by his own two fists and demand a following.

But David does something else:

> In the course of time, David inquired of the LORD. "Shall I go up to one of the towns of Judah?" he asked.
>
> The LORD said, "Go up."
>
> David asked, "Where shall I go?"
>
> "To Hebron," the LORD answered. (2 Samuel 2:1)

FROM FUGITIVE TO MONARCH

David remembers when Samuel anointed him so long ago and had whispered, "You will be the next king." Now David really wants to know: *Is it time?* And he takes that question to God. David doesn't rush to seize the throne and take charge over the whole nation all at once. He waits patiently on God for further instruction. Then God reveals His plan to him, and tells him to begin his reign in Hebron.

In those days the Lord spoke audibly to His servants. Today He speaks from His Word. You might be in a situation where you're wondering, *God has obviously opened a door, ready for me to walk through; but should I?* Our tendency can be to rush in when we see clear benefit to doing so. But sometimes it's better to pace our first steps with great care.

Here we see the Lord in essence telling David, "You're to be king, but be humble about It. Walk carefully. Be sensitive."

That's what David does. Following God's instruction, he goes to Hebron, where he has a limited reign over only a portion of the nation—the people of Judah, the tribe David belongs to by birth. "The length of time David was king in Hebron over Judah was seven years and six months" (2 Samuel 2:11). He settles in, knowing he has the ability to do more, to handle the entire nation—but only in God's time. David doesn't complain. He isn't anxious. He has learned to wait on God.

Elsewhere in the nation, there are self-appointed hotshots who've been riding on Saul's shirttails, waiting to make their move. So there's conflict between them and David's realm:

> The war between the house of Saul and the house of David lasted a long time. David grew stronger and stronger, while the house of Saul grew weaker and weaker. (3:1)

Unfortunately, while there in Hebron, David makes some decisions he will live to regret. We go on to read that "sons were born to David in Hebron" (3:2). There in 2 Samuel 3, what follows is a listing of six sons— and six mothers. David quickly produces six children by six different wives! And that's not even counting his first wife—Michal, Saul's daughter. Saul had given her to him after David defeated Goliath, but when David was later forced to flee for his life, Saul gave her to another man. (After Saul's death, David demands her back, despite her marriage to another.) Later, after David begins to rule from Jerusalem, even more wives and children will enter the family.

This polygamy is one of the dark spots in David's life, a weak side of his character that will come back to haunt him. If I count correctly, the biblical record gives us the names of twenty sons and one daughter born to David, and the names of eight wives. There are also other wives and children whose names we aren't given, as well as concubines (ten of these, unnamed, are mentioned in 2 Samuel 15:16). The size of David's immediate family is enormous! Keep all this in mind, because David's huge family becomes a thorny issue later, especially after his adultery with Bathsheba.

This sizable family gets off to a robust start during his years in Hebron. And it's there, in time, that his kingship over all the tribes of Israel, the entire nation, is finally consolidated:

> All the tribes of Israel came to David at Hebron and said, "We are your own flesh and blood. In the past, while Saul was king over us, you were the one who led Israel on their military campaigns. And the LORD said to you, 'You will shepherd my people Israel, and you will become their ruler.'"

When all the elders of Israel had come to King David at Hebron, the king made a covenant with them at Hebron before the LORD, and they anointed David king over Israel.

David was thirty years old when he became king, and he reigned forty years. In Hebron he reigned over Judah seven years and six months, and in Jerusalem he reigned over all Israel and Judah thirty-three years. (2 Samuel 5:1–5)

DAVID'S AUTHORITY

David displays his military leadership in making Jerusalem his head-quarters:

The king and his men marched to Jerusalem to attack the Jebusites, who lived there. The Jebusites said to David, "You will not get in here; even the blind and the lame can ward you off." . . . Nevertheless, David captured the fortress of Zion—which is the City of David. . . .

David then took up residence in the fortress and called it the City of David. He built up the area around it, from the terraces inward. And he became more and more powerful, because the LORD God Almighty was with him.

Now Hiram king of Tyre sent envoys to David, along with cedar logs and carpenters and stonemasons, and they built a palace for David. Then David knew that the LORD had established him as king over Israel and had exalted his kingdom for the sake of his people Israel. (5:6–12)

David finally has the limitless reign he'd been promised as God's anointed leader. He has great power and great blessing from God. Blessings overflow in David's cup. Few monarchs have known such remarkable power and prestige. Historian G. Frederick Owen described well this remarkable season of success for David's reign:

Everything favored national prosperity for Israel. There was no great power in Western Asia inclined to prevent her becoming a powerful monarchy. . . . The Hittites had been humbled; and Egypt, under the last kings of the twenty-first dynasty, had lost her prestige and had all but collapsed. The Philistines were driven to a narrow portion of their old dominion, and the king of Tyre sought friendly alliance with David.

With a steady hand David set out to force back and defeat Israel's enemies who had constantly crowded, horned, and harassed the Hebrews—Moab and Ammon were conquered; then the Edomites, alarmed at the ever-increasing power of Israel, rose against David, but were routed. . . . Commercial highways were thrown open, and in came merchandise, culture, and wealth from Phoenicia, Damascus, Assyria, Arabia, Egypt, and more distant lands. To his people, David was king, judge, and general, but to the nations round about, he was the leading power in all the Near Eastern world—the mightiest monarch of the day.[13]

That's a lot of clout for any leader to handle, especially for a man as passionate as David. Very few can be trusted with that kind of power, because with it come unique temptations that few can handle. As the famous saying goes, "Power corrupts, absolute power corrupts absolutely."

Remember, the hand of God is with David; nevertheless, he's still a man. He can still be prone to failure (more on that later). For now, David surely enjoys these blessings that have been a long time coming.

His accomplishments are marvelous. Territorially, David expands his nation's boundaries from six thousand square miles to sixty thousand. He sets up extensive trade routes that reach throughout the known world, and from them, wealth comes into Israel to an extent that the nation has never known.

David unifies the nation under Jehovah God, creating a national interest in spiritual things. He's not a priest but a king—yet he lifts up and strengthens the role of the priesthood so that Judaism can operate openly and freely in the land. He destroys pagan altars.

I say it again: David is a truly remarkable man and monarch—a brilliant organizer, a brilliant manager, a brilliant planner. He's also a man of brilliant battlefield savvy, who stays on the leading edge of military defense.

DAVID'S HUMAN FAILINGS

David is also human—very human. In fact, he has three major failures in his life, three heartbreaking disappointments.

First, he becomes so involved in public pursuits that he loses control of his family. The man has too many wives and too many children to lead and rear them properly. Being a man of virile passion, he gives himself passionately to these women—and the result is too many children thrown together to mostly raise themselves. When there's insufficient parental direction and guidance, there's little difference between life on the back street and life in the king's palace. A king or queen can produce prodigals and rebels just as easily as parents living in poverty.

And that's exactly what David produces. At the height of his reign, with all these impressive events and accomplishments happening nationally, it's evident that David has lost touch domestically. He has undisciplined children. As we'll see, his son Absalom will rebel, deceiving his father and actually pushing him off the throne. Tragically, David will flee like a wounded animal.

Another son, Amnon, will rape his own half sister, Tamar. This horrendous act leads to murder and enormous dysfunctional relationships within the royal family. According to the sacred text, David's only reaction to this is that he becomes angry. That's it. Perhaps his own sin and failure with Bathsheba prevents him from really knowing what to do—or else from doing what he knows is needed. Before the nation, David is decisive and brilliant; but behind the scenes, within the walls of his own home, he is passive and negligent.

We'll see also that in David's elderly years, his son Adonijah like Absalom—will also try to usurp the throne.

Another huge failure of David's at this time is that he indulges himself in extravagant extremes of passion. Whatever David does, he does with all his heart. When he fights, he fights to the bitter end, completely vanquishing the enemy. When he loves, he loves with all his heart—and those numerous wives and concubines are examples of this sexual passion.

His appetites will also lead to inappropriate seasons of leisure. He can be indolent, lazy, indifferent. One spring, at the time of year when kings go out to battle, David stays at home in Jerusalem. In his passion for leisure, there comes an infamous day when he falls into sin with Bathsheba. He is consumed with lust and brings Bathsheba to his bed. He then lies to people around him, and the lies lead eventually to murder. We'll look at all this later in greater detail.

J. Oswald Sanders summed it up correctly: "David's greatest fault lay in his yielding to passions of the flesh."[14]

David's third tragic failure at this time is that he becomes a victim of self-sufficiency and pride. In simple terms, David begins to believe his own track record. His pride will lead to an arrogant decision that earns swift judgment from God—and seventy thousand people will die. And this, too, we'll also explore closely.

TIMELESS TRUTHS

Here are two particularly timeless principles we can learn from David's reign that apply directly to our own lives. First, *no pursuit is more important than the cultivation of a godly family.* And second, *no character trait is more needed than genuine integrity.*

Although David will experience significant failures, when God measures the tree of David's life, He doesn't condemn it to be cut down for kindling. In His great love, mercy, and grace, the Lord honors the many efforts of this man on behalf of God's people and God's name, as well as the integrity of the man's heart.

Sometimes we need to take a good long look at areas in our lives that need attention—areas where we're particularly vulnerable to temptation. We need to ask the Lord to clear away those paths that have been scarred by the wreckage of yesterday. We need to be people of integrity who care enough about yesterday to make it right with our children today.

There's no person or righteous cause that the enemy of our souls will not try to destroy, and he loves to multiply his victories. If David were with us today, I believe he would tell us to beware—to remember that the devil is always lurking, relentlessly seeking to destroy.

LESSONS TO LEARN—AT DAVID'S EXPENSE

Three lessons linger as I think through this time in David's life.

1. *Prosperity and ease are perilous times, not merely blessings.* C. S. Lewis's *Screwtape Letters* mentions "the long, dull, monotonous years of middle-aged prosperity," which are shown to be excellent campaign weather for the devil.[15]

Have you hit a prosperous season when you don't have to worry too much about many things that used to demand a lot of attention? Take heed! More often than not, prosperity and ease are perilous times.

2. *Gross sin is a culmination of a process, not a sudden act.* Early on in Hebron, King David is already amassing a number of wives. But when will enough be enough? When he has a full harem, he still isn't satisfied but is driven by lust for more. Gross sin isn't a sudden action; it's a process that culminates. And one who commits gross sin often tells himself later, *I can't believe I did that.* That's certainly what David must be saying.

3. Confession and repentance help heal a wound—but they'll never erase all the scars. If we're honest enough to admit it, there are times when we sin and think, I can do this now and confess and repent later, and God will forgive me. And that's true. But I must warn you, you can never erase the scars. He will heal the wound, but He'll leave the scars. And your children may suffer as a result, and their children after them. That's the heartache of it all. Sin has terrible wages.

The only hope we have is daily dependence on the living Lord. It's the only way we can make it. He's compassionate toward our experience of infirmity, weakness, and inability in the dark and lonely times to say no. He's touched by that. And He says, "I'm ready with all the power you need. Call on Me, and I'll give you what you need."

So stop this moment and call on Him. He will hear and heed our cry. I know this—in recent days I've done just that, and He has provided the strength I needed to go on.

GOING AFTER GOD'S OWN HEART: From David's Psalm 139, make his prayer your own:

> Search me, God, and know my heart;
> test me and know my anxious thoughts.
> See if there is any offensive way in me,
> and lead me in the way everlasting. (139:23–24)

CHAPTER 13

FAILING TO DO HIS HOMEWORK

When someone mentions David, most people think immediately of David and Goliath, of David the warrior. They may also think of David the prolific psalm-writer, or David and Jonathan together as the model of close friendship.

They may also think of David the sinner—in his adultery with Bathsheba. As a father, I'm often drawn to picture David as a grieving, broken man, dissolving in tears (as we'll see later) upon hearing of the untimely death of his son Absalom.

But in the New Testament, God emphasizes something else in how David is remembered. In Paul's first sermon recorded in the book of Acts, he gave an overview of how God guided Israel's history (leading up to the coming of Christ)—and he mentioned a truth we discussed earlier:

"Then the people asked for a king, and he [God] gave them Saul son of Kish, of the tribe of Benjamin, who ruled forty years. After removing Saul, he made David their king. God testified concerning him: 'I have found David son of Jesse, *a man after my own heart; he will do everything I want him to do.*'" (Acts 13:21–22)

God doesn't say He found David to be a great warrior, or a faithful shepherd, or a brilliant king—but rather, in essence, "a man to care about the things I care about, a man whose heart beats in sync with Mine, and who'll do what I've created him to do."

David puts his focus where God puts His. That's being a person after God's own heart.

To people like that, nothing in their relationship with God is insignificant. They keep short accounts; if they stray from Him, they don't get far before they face up to where they are and correct their course. They come back in line quickly, because they're after His heart. They're hot after God, highly motivated to obey God's *precepts* and to honor His *principles*. Here's the distinction between those two words: When you're driving and see a sign that says "Speed Limit 35," that's a precept. If the sign reads, "Drive Carefully," that's a principle—it means one thing in heavy urban traffic, and something entirely different along a lonely road out on the prairie. You use wisdom to apply the principle appropriately.

When it comes to the spiritual life, those who are after God in their hearts will care as much about the principles as they do about the precepts. When they come across a precept that's clearly delineated, they say, "I see that my life doesn't conform to that precept—I need to bring my life in line." And they do just that.

That's what David does in what we see next in his life. It's a classic example of his being a man after God's heart.

DAVID'S CONCERN: THE PEOPLE'S RIGHT WORSHIP

In the latter part of a forty-year reign, King Saul had compromised and fiddled around with all kinds of things besides his job. In particular—and unlike David—he neglected the things of God.

There was, for example, the sad situation with the ark of the covenant.

Ever since the Israelites left Egypt, their central place of worship has been the tabernacle—the tent structure (God Himself had given its original blueprint to Moses) where the ark of the covenant was meant to be kept. Under Saul's weak and negligent reign, interest in the tabernacle had waned. The piece of holy furniture known as the ark of the covenant had earlier become separated from the tabernacle—in fact, the Philistines had earlier captured it and held it for a time in their territory. But now it's in a place called Baalah (also known as Kiriath Jearim), about seven or eight miles from Jerusalem. For twenty years it has been kept there in the house of a man named Abinadab.

In those days, the absence of the ark from the tabernacle meant that the presence of God had departed, because the Lord dwelt in His glory upon the ark of the covenant within the tabernacle. The ark was so important to the Lord that He gave Moses specific details for how to build it. It was to be portable, so the Israelites could move this house of God through the wilderness and into the land of Canaan as their central place of worship.

It was the holiest place on earth. Everywhere the ark of the covenant was placed, God's glory—the light, the *shekinah* glory of God—rested on the ark of the covenant. That laser-like ray from heaven was central to the worship of Jehovah, since it represented His presence.

This ark itself was a rectangular box or chest made of wood, gold-plated inside and out. Inside the ark were three objects: a golden jar containing manna from the wilderness, Aaron's ancient rod, and the stone tablets of the covenant. On top of the ark was a gold covering called the mercy seat, and overlooking this were two cherubim of hammered gold with outstretched wings of gold. They faced each other, one on either end of the ark. God had promised that He would meet with His people there between these golden angelic creatures looking down over the mercy seat. To be sure, this piece of furniture was absolutely holy, set apart to God.

All this sounds strange to us, since our worship patterns today are quite different, ever since Christ came and died and was resurrected. Back then, so many things of God were expressed in symbols and types and pictures—like looking through smoked or foggy glass; you could see shapes, but not the details.

When David takes over the throne, he realizes that the ark of the covenant isn't around, and thus there's no central place of worship for the nation. The people's spiritual life has therefore become mediocre. Their heart is anything but hot after God. David knows he needs to put that piece of sacred furniture back in its rightful place, setting it up as God designed it. His heart is after God's heart, even on the matter of locating a small piece of sacred furniture and getting it in the right place. For David, no detail related to worshiping God is unimportant.

Now God had been very careful with His instructions about how the ark was to be carried. At the base of each of the ark's four corners, a gold ring was fixed, and through these rings were gold-plated poles; by these poles resting on the shoulder of those carrying it, the ark could be lifted and moved without any human hand ever touching the ark itself.

Also, God had clearly stated that only Levites were to handle all the tabernacle furniture, including the ark. Every aspect of Israel's worship was important to God—even how the ark was transported from one place to another.

And that's where David gets into trouble. David is an expedient man, a pragmatist. After all, he's the king, the decision maker. He knows that to get the ark of the covenant down the hillside home of Abinadab in Baalah, the quickest and best way to do it is on a cart. So David launches his own plan to bring the ark of the covenant to Jerusalem. He has his men set the ark on a new cart, and essentially tells a few of them, "Haul it down to Jerusalem":

> David again brought together all the able young men of Israel—thirty thousand. He and all his men went to Baalah in Judah to bring up from there the ark of God, which is called by the Name, the name of the LORD Almighty, who is enthroned between the cherubim on the ark. They set the ark of God on a new cart and brought it from the house of Abinadab, which was on the hill. Uzzah and Ahio, sons of Abinadab, were guiding the new cart with the ark of God on it, and Ahio was walking in front of it. (2 Samuel 6:1–4)

The plan is going well, and David and the people are thrilled:

> David and all Israel were celebrating with all their might before the LORD, with castanets, harps, lyres, timbrels, sistrums and cymbals. (6:5)

So here's David, rejoicing—with the delight of obedience beating in his heart. He knows that the ark is coming back home where it belonged in Zion.

THE FALLOUT

Then something dreadful happens:

> When they came to the threshing floor of Nakon, Uzzah reached out
> and took hold of the ark of God, because the oxen stumbled. The Lord's
> anger burned against Uzzah because of his irreverent act; therefore God
> struck him down, and he died there beside the ark of God. (6:6–7)

Uzzah reaches out to steady the ark so it won't fall—that's all he does.
And isn't it the practical thing to do, rather than let the ark fall off the cart
and be damaged or broken open?

However, the ark would not have been in any danger of falling if they
were carrying it exactly as God had commanded. The Levites—God's chosen men for this task—were to carry the ark on their shoulders using the
poles that slid through the gold rings at the ark's base. But David is trying
a more convenient method.

There's an old saying that gets tossed around in certain situations: "It
doesn't matter what you do; just do *something*, even if it's wrong!" That is
stupid counsel. If you don't know what's right to do, wait until you know—
then do it with all your might. That's wise counsel.

David is telling himself, We need to get the ark where it belongs; who
cares how we do it, so long as we get it there?

God cares, David. And to prove it, He takes Uzzah's life.

David is there, standing alongside Uzzah's corpse, and he gets mad:
"David was angry because the Lord's wrath had broken out against Uzzah"
(6:8). More importantly, however, the Lord was angry at David for not taking His Word seriously.

Being a man after God's heart doesn't mean you're perfect. But when
you see you're wrong, you face it. You own up. You come to terms with it.
And that's what David presses into: "David was afraid of the Lord that day
and said, 'How can the ark of the Lord ever come to me?'" (6:9).

The problem is that David hasn't done his homework. When any of us
make that mistake, we often get into trouble. And the Lord is telling us,
"Look, I want you to take counsel from Me, from My Book. If you want

to have a heart like Mine, then check My Word, and you'll find either a precept or a principle that relates to whatever decision you're facing. Then proceed according to what you read—and I'll give you joy you can't believe. But if you disobey—you'll be miserable."

Uzzah is taken from the earth because he touches an ultra-holy article of furniture that is not to be touched, especially by a non-Levite. Who cares about Levites? God does. Who cares about golden poles through golden rings as a way to transport the ark? God does. If He didn't care, He wouldn't have said anything about it. Because *He* cares, *we* also must care.

That's the whole point here. When we begin to care about the things God cares about, we become people after His heart. Only then do we begin to have real freedom and real happiness.

David's fear of the Lord brings his plan to a halt:

> He was not willing to take the ark of the LORD to be with him in the City of David. Instead, he took it to the house of Obed-Edom the Gittite. (6:10)

Months pass. There's still no ark in Jerusalem. David, with his stomach churning, is wondering what's next. He wants the ark of the Lord in Jerusalem, but Obed-Edom has it at his house.

And Obed-Edom is having the time of his life:

> The ark of the LORD remained in the house of Obed-Edom the Gittite for three months, and the LORD blessed him and his entire household. Now King David was told, "The LORD has blessed the household of Obed-Edom and everything he has, because of the ark of God."
>
> So David went to bring up the ark of God from the house of Obed-Edom to the City of David with rejoicing. (6:11–12)

In a parallel passage from 1 Chronicles, we read more details of how David chooses this time "to bring up the ark of God":

> David . . . prepared a place for the ark of God and pitched a tent for it. Then David said, "No one but the Levites may carry the ark of God,

because the LORD chose them to carry the ark of the LORD and to minister before him forever."

David assembled all Israel in Jerusalem to bring up the ark of the LORD to the place he had prepared for it. He called together the descendants of Aaron and the Levites. . . . Then David summoned Zadok and Abiathar the priests, and Uriel, Asaiah, Joel, Shemaiah, Eliel and Amminadab the Levites. He said to them, "You are the heads of the Levitical families; you and your fellow Levites are to consecrate yourselves and bring up the ark of the LORD, the God of Israel, to the place I have prepared for it. It was because you, the Levites, did not bring it up the first time that the LORD our God broke out in anger against us. We did not inquire of him about how to do it in the prescribed way."

So the priests and Levites consecrated themselves in order to bring up the ark of the LORD, the God of Israel. And the Levites carried the ark of God with the poles on their shoulders, as Moses had commanded in accordance with the word of the LORD. (1 Chronicles 15:1–15)

What's the big deal about carrying the ark the right way? What's the big message for us? The message is about our life. The small details of obeying God can drive us crazy. We don't want to take the time; it's a lot easier to just be quick and practical. Besides, the Lord can't be that concerned about minor details, right?

Wrong!

If the Lord cared enough to write precepts and principles for our lives, and He cared enough to preserve these writings for our lasting instruction—then He cares enough about the details to have you and me pull them off precisely His way.

That's ultimately what David does, and I love that about him:

When those who were carrying the ark of the LORD had taken six steps, he [David] sacrificed a bull and a fattened calf. Wearing a linen ephod, David was dancing before the LORD with all his might, while he and all Israel were bringing up the ark of the LORD with shouts and the sound of trumpets. (2 Samuel 6:13–15)

David and the people get so excited about this because now they're free. When you obey, you're free; when you disobey, you're in bondage.

But I should warn you: When you're really free, people who aren't so free will have trouble with your freedom. We see that on this occasion in the behavior of Michal, David's first wife.

Picture it: Her husband is down there dancing and singing and shouting, while Michal is up in a second-floor flat, frowning down on her husband.

> As the ark of the LORD was entering the City of David, Michal daughter of Saul watched from a window. And when she saw King David leaping and dancing before the LORD, she despised him in her heart. (6:16)

David is rejoicing *in obedience to God*. He offers burnt offerings and blesses the people. He distributes food to the people in celebration.

Then, in ecstasy, he goes home—"David returned home to bless his household" (6:20). He walks up the stairs and opens the door—and hears this from his wife Michal:

> "How the king of Israel has distinguished himself today, going around half-naked in full view of the slave girls of his servants as any vulgar fellow would!" (6:20)

Sarcasm! Jab, jab, jab. This couple does not have good chemistry. (They should never have married.)

Notice how David responds; he refuses to let her reaction win the day:

> David said to Michal, "It was before the LORD, who chose me rather than your father or anyone from his house when he appointed me ruler over the LORD's people Israel—I will celebrate before the LORD. I will become even more undignified than this, and I will be humiliated in my own eyes. But by these slave girls you spoke of, I will be held in honor."
> And Michal daughter of Saul had no children to the day of her death. (6:21–23)

David gets in a dig at Michal with his reference to her father—but he's stating relevant truth. David's eyes are on the Lord; Michal's eyes are on other people. When those opposites mix, an explosion is sure to occur.

We don't know exactly why Michal never has children. Perhaps David is never again intimate with her. Whatever the reason, she's forever barren—a weighty stigma for any Jewish woman to endure.

LESSONS WORTH REMEMBERING

Two things here strike me especially in this experience of David, both having to do with the matter of focus.

1. *The better you know where you stand with the Lord, the freer you can be.* When you do the homework, when you find out where you stand with your Lord, and you follow His plan—then you're truly free. You'll be misunderstood by some, of course. And some will detest you, like Michal with David. But you won't care that much about it; you'll care about the Lord's opinion. There's no freedom like the kind He provides. In a word, it's *grace.*

2. *The freer you are before the Lord, the more confident you'll become.* When you know where you stand—that's real security.

If you're becoming increasingly concerned about God's fine print regarding your life, I want to commend you and encourage you. People like you make godly wives and godly husbands, and godly roommates, and godly workers, and godly professionals, and godly pastors, and godly musicians. You care enough about your life that regardless of your occupation, when you hear something declared from Scripture, you're thinking, *How can I get that into my life?* Good for you! Don't stop. Don't even slow down.

There was a period in my own life when I dinked around with the Christian life. I took some, and left some. I bit off the part that was tasty, but turned away from the part that was painful.

Then one man cared enough to tell me the truth: "You're a classic illustration of a heady Christian." I considered this an insult. I was so proud, I didn't want to listen to anything else he had to say. But he went on: "Before you walk away I want tell you that you have the makings of putting it together. But you're a long ways from it." Then he offered to stick around me for a number of months and help me in the process, so I could see how to "put it together," whether in public or private. He cared enough for me to do that. Those were some tough years in my life.

Like you, I'm still in the process of putting it together. But thank God for that friend who helped me get started—to begin putting those precepts to work in my life, and to quit excusing my disobedience.

Knowing where you stand before the Lord leads to true freedom. Being free before the Lord, you'll become confident—and that's genuine security.

Maybe the Lord has clearly led you to do something, but you're resisting: *No, not now.* Maybe you're trying to bargain with Him, substituting something else in place of His direct advice. Listen to me: Wait no longer. Obey today!

Maybe you have a streak of stubborn pride—you've bragged about your strong will as you've cultivated the habit of resistance. Listen to me: Rebel no more. Obey today!

Or maybe you've developed a deceitful technique of hiding your disobedience behind the mask of lies, or rationalization, or manipulation, or blame. Listen to me: Deceive no further. Obey today!

The only real proof of your love for your Lord is obedience. Nothing more, nothing less, nothing else.

———————

GOING AFTER GOD'S OWN HEART: From David's Psalm 40, make his prayer your own:

> I desire to do your will, my God;
> your law is within my heart. . . .
> Be pleased to save me, LORD;
> come quickly, LORD, to help me. (40:8,13)

CHAPTER 14

WHEN GOD SAYS NO

Being a courageous warrior, David is often involved in battle and stressful situations. However, there now comes a rare interlude of calm and quiet in his life: "The king was settled in his palace and the LORD had given him rest from all his enemies around him" (2 Samuel 7:1).

David has seldom known this kind of peace. The age-old battle with the Philistines is temporarily settled; all is quiet, at least for a while. There's not another Goliath on the scene shouting blasphemies.

Inside his lovely cedar-lined home, David begins to reflect. An idea—a longing and a dream, really—comes to mind. To get feedback on this idea, David goes to the prophet Nathan, a close friend and counselor.

> He said to Nathan the prophet, "Here I am, living in a house of cedar, while the ark of God remains in a tent."
>
> Nathan replied to the king, "Whatever you have in mind, go ahead and do it, for the LORD is with you." (7:2–3)

Good friends offer encouragement, and Nathan encourages David to follow through on what's in his heart. And what exactly is that?

We've seen David bring the ark of God into Jerusalem for the people of Israel in their worship. But David begins to be bothered by the fact that the ark's home is only a tent, while David himself lives in a beautiful palace. He has it in mind to build a permanent residence for God, to house the ark and all the sacred furniture. In all the centuries since the nation of Israel left Egypt, God's dwelling place has been the tabernacle rather than any permanent structure, but David desires to change that. *I want to build a house for God, a temple in His honor.*

From everything we know about David, he has no ulterior motive here, no selfish ambition, no desire to make a name for himself. In building this house, he genuinely wants to exalt no other name but Jehovah's.

In the quieter interludes of our life, we often have time for our mind to seize a dream or an ideal. In a quiet moment you may have realized the vocation into which God was calling you. It's in the interludes of life that those things often happen. You have to slow down and become quiet in those special times to hear His voice, to sense His leading.

But let me add this: Sometimes your dream is from God, and sometimes not, and it's often hard to determine which is which. Your dream may be noble and worthy in itself, but when it's not of God, it won't come to fulfillment. Nor should it.

You may have trusted friends who say, as Nathan did to David, "Go for it, do all that's in your mind; the Lord is surely in this"—only to have God show you later that the dream is *not* His plan.

That's what happens to David.

GOD REDIRECTS

Look at God's response. Though it's communicated to David through Nathan, it's coming straight from God:

> That night the word of the LORD came to Nathan, saying: "Go and tell my servant David, 'This is what the LORD says: Are you the one to build me a house to dwell in?'" (2 Samuel 7:4–5)

A parallel passage puts it more directly: "Go and tell my servant David, 'This is what the LORD says: *You are not the one* to build me a house to dwell in'" (1 Chronicles 17:3–4).

What a hard answer for Nathan to take to the king! Just hours earlier, he encouraged David to go ahead and pursue his plans. Now Nathan hears the Lord saying, "No, no!"

But even while halting David's dream, God offers him personal affirmation—again through Nathan:

> "This is what the LORD Almighty says: I took you from the pasture, from tending the flock, and appointed you ruler over my people Israel. I have been with you wherever you have gone, and I have cut off all your enemies from before you." (2 Samuel 7:8–9)

What the Lord is saying is clear. "David, with My choosing, My gifting, and My presence—I've made you Israel's king. Your purpose from Me has been to *lead My people*—not to build a temple." God is confirming David's true calling: "You're a man of war. Your heart's on the battlefield. You're a soldier, a fighter—not a builder. And I've blessed you in this, so that all your enemies have been subdued."

Then come words of promise—personally for David, and nationally for Israel:

> "Now I will make your name great, like the names of the greatest men on earth. And I will provide a place for my people Israel and will plant them so that they can have a home of their own and no longer be disturbed. Wicked people will not oppress them anymore, as they did at the beginning and have done ever since the time I appointed leaders over my people Israel. I will also give you rest from all your enemies." (7:9–11)

Then—astoundingly—an even higher promise to David:

> "The LORD declares to you that *the* LORD *himself will establish a house for you*: When your days are over and you rest with your ancestors, I will raise up your offspring to succeed you, your own flesh and blood, and I will establish his kingdom. He is the one who will build a house for my Name, and I will establish the throne of his kingdom forever." (7:11–13)

What a breakthrough! "David, you are going to know the delight of having your own son build this temple! The dream will be fulfilled—not through your efforts but through those of your son."

Keep in mind that it's not a question of God's judgment coming upon David as a consequence of sin on his part. It's simply God's redirecting David's plan—and saying, "I say no to you and yes to your son. Now accept that."

And now—notice especially the first sentence in those words of promise from the Lord: Instead of David constructing a "house" (the temple) for the Lord, the Lord promises to "establish a house"—to provide and sustain a royal dynasty—for David. Incredibly, it's a lineage that will last *forever*. That's God's promise.

As we now know, this kingly line of David's offspring will culminate in the eternal King of kings—Jesus, called "the Son of David." There could be no greater "house," no greater heritage for any man! And it's promised by the Lord to the man after His own heart—to David in his humility before God.

But was it wrong or misguided of David in the first place to want to build the temple himself?

Look for a moment at a revealing passage in 2 Chronicles. David's son Solomon is speaking here, years after his father's death:

> "My father David had it in his heart to build a temple for the Name of the LORD, the God of Israel. But the LORD said to my father David, 'You did *well* to have it in your heart to build a temple for my Name. Nevertheless, you are not the one to build the temple, but your son, your own flesh and blood—he is the one who will build the temple for my Name.'" (2 Chronicles 6:7–9)

David "did well" in his desire to erect the temple; God commends him for that. So this is not a matter of David being wrong. Rather, it's for him to accept God's *no* regarding this matter, and to live with the mystery of His will.

So often we expect God to package His plan for us exactly as we envision. We want our logic to be His logic. When it isn't, we wonder what's wrong when our life isn't working out like we've planned and hoped. But when God tells us no, it isn't necessarily discipline or rejection. It may simply be *redirection*. You've pursued His will—that's your consistent desire. With all good intentions you once determined that by God's grace you were going to pursue this or that direction in life. But here you are, perhaps many years later, and it hasn't worked out.

Sometimes that puts us on a guilt trip. Others might even tell you, "You're out of God's will." More likely, the very road you're traveling is His will for you, and it took His saying no about something else to get you on this right road.

In our walk with God, we have to listen carefully day to day. Revisit your life's work and calling each day. Keep it fresh, keep the fire hot; keep saying, "Lord, if this isn't Your arrangement, Your plan, then make me sensitive to that. Help me see whenever You want to redirect my steps."

As we see with David, God doesn't call everyone to build temples. He calls some people to be soldiers, to do the work in the trenches. God has all kinds of creative ways to use us—including ways we can't even imagine. And we certainly can't see around the next bend in the road.

Let me also add that one of the hardest things to take is when God is using someone else to accomplish what you thought was *your* objective. That's what David has to hear: "It won't be you, David, to build My temple; it will be your son, Solomon."

A BEAUTIFUL RESPONSE

David's response to all this is beautiful in its humility, gratefulness, and awe. Notice first his posture, and how he addresses the Lord with childlike wonder:

> Then King David went in and sat before the LORD, and he said: "Who am I, Sovereign LORD, and what is my family, that you have brought me this far?" (2 Samuel 7:18)

Who am I—to be so blessed! You know, it's important for each of us to occasionally sit down and take a long look at our short lives—and count our blessings. *Who am I, Lord, that You should give me all this? Who am I?*

As David's prayer goes forward, he says nothing about the temple, the "house" for the Lord that he's been longing to build. God's words to him have redirected his attention to a different "house," an eternal one—and David's fully on board with that. The man after God's heart is overwhelmed with worshipful wonder about this promised blessing, and about what it means for God's people. Notice how often he mentions it in this prayer:

"And as if this were not enough in your sight, Sovereign LORD, you have also spoken about the future of *the house of your servant*—and *this decree*, Sovereign LORD, is for a mere human!

"What more can David say to you? For you know your servant, Sovereign LORD. For the sake of your word and according to your will, *you have done this great thing* and made it known to your servant.

"How great you are, Sovereign LORD! . . . You have established your people Israel as your very own forever, and you, LORD, have become their God.

"And now, LORD God, keep forever the promise you have made concerning *your servant and his house*. Do as you promised, so that your name will be great forever. Then people will say, 'The LORD Almighty is God over Israel!' And *the house of your servant David* will be established in your sight.

"LORD Almighty, God of Israel, you have revealed this to your servant, saying, '*I will build a house for you.*' So your servant has found courage to pray this prayer to you. Sovereign LORD, you are God! Your covenant is trustworthy, and you have promised *these good things* to your servant. Now be pleased to *bless the house of your servant*, that it may continue forever in your sight; for you, Sovereign LORD, have spoken, and with your *blessing the house of your servant* will be blessed forever." (2 Samuel 7:19–29)

What a powerful statement this is, especially after what must have been a moment of keen disappointment for David.

And jumping ahead, we find that he thoroughly and unselfishly supports his son in this building project that has been David's own dream:

David said, "My son Solomon is young and inexperienced, and the house to be built for the LORD should be of great magnificence and fame and splendor in the sight of all the nations. Therefore I will make preparations for it." So *David made extensive preparations before his death.* (1 Chronicles 22:5)

And we read this about some of those preparations:

So David . . . appointed stonecutters to prepare dressed stone for building the house of God. He provided a large amount of iron to make nails for the doors of the gateways and for the fittings, and more bronze than could be weighed. He also provided more cedar logs than could be counted. (22:2–4)

David will himself confess to Solomon, "I have taken great pains to provide for the temple of the LORD" (22:14). And then, "David ordered all the leaders of Israel to help his son Solomon" (22:17).

David may have been weak as a father at earlier times—but in this moment, he stands tall.

HOPE FOR BROKEN DREAMS

For us, I see two simple but important truths in all this.

1. *When God tells us no, it means He has a better way.* And He expects us to support it.

2. *Our best reaction to this is cooperation and humility.* He doesn't call everybody to build the temple, but He does call everyone to be faithful and obedient.

Do you identify with David? You may be living with broken dreams. Sometime in the past, you had high hopes that your life would go in a certain direction. But the Lord, for some mysterious reason, has said no. Perhaps you've made well-prepared plans, only to see them crumble at your feet. Now you're empty-handed. You move along in life, and may even find yourself becoming shelved, while others take charge of what you had wanted to be responsible for.

I want to tell you that God is ready to fill your empty hands, more than you could imagine—if you'll only lift those hands to Him in obedience and praise, as David did. God is still alive and well, and He knows what He's doing.

Whether He says yes or no to your plans and dreams, His answer is best, and never wrong.

GOING AFTER GOD'S OWN HEART: From David's Psalm 27, make his prayer your own:

> One thing I ask from the LORD,
> this only do I seek:
> that I may dwell in the house of the LORD
> all the days of my life,
> to gaze on the beauty of the LORD
> and to seek him in his temple.
> For in the day of trouble
> he will keep me safe in his dwelling;
> he will hide me in the shelter of his sacred tent
> and set me high upon a rock. (27:4–5)

CHAPTER 15

GRACE IN A BARREN PLACE

The word *grace* means many things to many people.

We refer to a ballet dancer as having grace. We say grace at meals. We talk about certain admired women who bring grace to any room they enter. Grace can mean coordination of movement, it can mean a prayer, it can refer to dignity and elegance.

Most importantly, grace can mean unmerited favor—extending special favor to someone who doesn't deserve it, hasn't earned it, and can never repay it. In Scripture we come across scenes that beautifully illustrate that kind of grace, and we stand amazed.

We find one of those moments now in the life of David. In my opinion, it's the greatest illustration of grace in the Old Testament. It involves an obscure man with an almost unpronounceable name. As we explore the story together, I hope you find it to be beautiful and unforgettable.

POSITIVE, UNCONDITIONAL ACCEPTANCE

As we've seen in the account of the Philistine slaughter of Saul's army on Mount Gilboa, among the dead that day was Jonathan, David's closest friend.

In the interlude of peace and quietness that David eventually experienced, as he spends time remembering the abundance of blessings he's known, I'm sure he thinks specifically about his love for Jonathan—and also about the tragic life of Saul, Jonathan's father. While reflecting in this way, David recalls a promise he made. He ponders this promise—and he addresses it.

> David asked, "Is there anyone still left of the house of Saul to whom I can show kindness for Jonathan's sake?" (2 Samuel 9:1)

That word *kindness* is there in most English Bible translations of this verse, but the original Hebrew word, *hesed*, can appropriately be rendered here as "grace." David's saying, "To whom I can show *grace* for Jonathan's sake." Grace is positive and unconditional acceptance of another person. Grace is a demonstration of love that's undeserved, unearned, and unrepayable.

So David ponders: Is there anybody around to whom I can demonstrate this kind of positive acceptance, this kind of love, for the sake of my friend Jonathan?

Why does David want to do this? Because he made a promise. In fact, two promises.

Back in 1 Samuel 20, when David, though destined for the throne, was still running for his life from King Saul, Saul's son Jonathan said this to David:

> "If my father intends to harm you, may the LORD deal with Jonathan, be it ever so severely, if I do not let you know and send you away in peace. May the LORD be with you as he has been with my father. But *show me unfailing kindness* like the LORD's kindness as long as I live, so that I may not be killed." (20:13–14)

It was the custom in Eastern dynasties that when a new king took over, family members of the previous dynasty were exterminated to take away the possibility of revolt. That's why Jonathan was asking David—who's certain to attain the throne—to show grace to Jonathan, and by extension to his family. *Will you preserve our lives?*

Without hesitation, David agreed. His love and commitment toward

Jonathan prompted him in that moment to enter into a binding covenant with his friend:

> So Jonathan made a covenant with the house of David, saying, "May the Lord call David's enemies to account." And Jonathan had David reaffirm his oath out of love for him, because he loved him as he loved himself. (20:16–17)

Later, you may recall, after David spared Saul's life in the cave, Saul said this to him:

> "I know that you will surely be king and that the kingdom of Israel will be established in your hands. Now swear to me by the Lord that you will not kill off my descendants or wipe out my name from my father's family."
>
> So David gave his oath to Saul. Then Saul returned home, but David and his men went up to the stronghold. (24:20–22)

David's promise, as we see, was to both Jonathan and Saul.

Now, after both their deaths, we find David thinking about that promise, and making inquiries. It's worth noting that David asks, "Is there *anyone* . . . ?" (2 Samuel 9:1). Not, "Is there anyone qualified?" Or, "Is there anyone worthy?" Regardless of who they are, is *anyone* still living who ought to be the recipient of David's unqualified acceptance based on unconditional love?

Well—they identify someone.

> Now there was a servant of Saul's household named Ziba. They summoned him to appear before David, and the king said to him, "Are you Ziba?"
>
> "At your service," he replied.
>
> The king asked, "Is there no one still alive from the house of Saul to whom I can show God's kindness?"
>
> Ziba answered the king, "There is still a son of Jonathan; he is lame in both feet." (2 Samuel 9:2–3)

Reading between the lines, we sense an implication in Ziba's words: "Yes, there's someone—but he's crippled. So, David, you should think twice about this, because the guy's not going to look right in your court. He won't fit the royal surroundings."

David's response is beautiful. He simply asks, "Where is he?" (9:4). David presses onward. He doesn't ask, "How badly disabled is he?" Nor does he ask how he got in that condition. He just wants to know where this man is located.

That's the way grace is. It isn't picky. Grace doesn't look for the deserving. Grace operates apart from the response or the ability of the recipient. Grace is one-sided. I repeat: Grace is God giving Himself in full acceptance to someone who does not deserve it and can never earn it and will never be able to repay.

This is what makes the story of David and Mephibosheth so memorable. A strong and famous king stoops down and reaches out to someone who represents everything David is not—this lame grandson of Saul.

So, where is he? Ziba answers: "He is at the house of Makir son of Ammiel in Lo Debar" (9:4).

That geographical term is interesting. *Lo* in Hebrew means "no," and *debar* is from the root word meaning "pasture or pastureland." So this descendant of Jonathan is in a place without pasture—some obscure, barren field in Palestine. He has hidden himself away in order to not be exterminated, as the custom was when dynasties changed. The only person who knows his whereabouts is an old servant of Saul, a man named Ziba.

Although David doesn't ask how this man became "lame in both feet," you and I are curious—and we find the answer elsewhere, in 2 Samuel 4. The story adds to the pathos of the situation:

Jonathan son of Saul had a son who was lame in both feet. He was five years old when the news about Saul and Jonathan [the news about their deaths in battle against the Philistines] came from Jezreel. His nurse picked him up and fled, but as she hurried to leave, he fell and became disabled. His name was Mephibosheth. (4:4)

As a result of that fall, this Mephibosheth is permanently disabled. He has been hiding away ever since, fearful for his life. The last thing he wants is to have an emissary from the king rap on his door. But that's exactly what happens.

Can you imagine his shock? We don't know how old Mephibosheth is, but he probably has a family of his own by now, for later we read that he has a young son himself.

As his door opens, Mephibosheth is looking into the faces of David's soldiers, who say, "The king wants to see you." Mephibosheth most likely thinks, *Well, this is the end.*

These men take him to Jerusalem, into the very presence of the king.

> And Mephibosheth the son of Jonathan, son of Saul, came to David and fell on his face and paid homage. And David said, "Mephibosheth!"
> And he answered, "Behold, I am your servant." (2 Samuel 9:6 ESV)

What a scary moment this must be. This impaired man lays aside his crutches and falls down before the king who has sovereign rights over his life. And the king shouts his name. Mephibosheth surely is expecting the worst.

> And David said to him, "Do not fear, for I will show you kindness for the sake of your father Jonathan, and I will restore to you all the land of Saul your father, and you shall eat at my table always." (9:7)

Can you imagine the feeling that comes over Mephibosheth in this moment? Expecting a sword to strike his neck, instead he hears unbelievable news from his king: He's to be given a place of honor at the king's table—like a member of the royal family.

What is this? So impossible to believe!

> Mephibosheth bowed down and said, "What is your servant, that you should notice a dead dog like me?" (9:8)

It gets better. David says more, confirming that this radical change for Mephibosheth is real:

Then the king summoned Ziba, Saul's steward, and said to him, "I have given your master's grandson everything that belonged to Saul and his family. You and your sons and your servants are to farm the land for him and bring in the crops, so that your master's grandson may be provided for. And Mephibosheth, grandson of your master, will always eat at my table." . . .

Then Ziba said to the king, "Your servant will do whatever my lord the king commands his servant to do." So Mephibosheth ate at David's table like one of the king's sons. . . .

And Mephibosheth lived in Jerusalem, because he always ate at the king's table; he was lame in both feet. (9:9–13)

What a magnificent demonstration of what grace is all about!

Picture what life will be like for him in years to come at David's supper table. The meal is set out and the dinner bell rings, and into the room come family members and guests. David's son Amnon, clever and witty, comes to the table first. Then there's the military commander (and David's nephew) Joab as a guest—muscular, masculine, his skin bronzed from the sun, walking tall and erect like the experienced soldier he is. Next comes David's son Absalom. Talk about handsome! From the crown of his head to the soles of his feet there's not a blemish on him. Then there's Tamar—beautiful, tender daughter of David. And later on, young Solomon will enter as well, the brilliant one. They all make their way to the table.

Then they hear this *clump, clump, clump*—here comes Mephibosheth, hobbling along. He smiles and humbly joins the others as he takes his place at the table like one of the king's sons.

And the tablecloth of grace covers his deformed feet. What a scene!

THE EXTENT OF GRACE

But that isn't the end of the story. That story is still going on, reflected in the lives of all God's children. I can think of at least eight analogies to indicate this.

1. *Mephibosheth as a young child surely enjoyed an intimate relationship*

with his father Jonathan. So also for the first man Adam, who enjoyed uninterrupted fellowship with his Creator-Father, and walked with the Lord in the cool of the evening.

2. *When disaster came, the nurse fled in fear and Mephibosheth suffered a fall.* It left him disabled for the rest of his days, and he went into hiding. Likewise, when sin came, Adam and Eve hid in fear. The first response of humanity was to hide from God, to find reasons for not being with God. As a result, all of humanity became spiritual invalids, and will always be so on earth.

3. *David, the king, out of sheer love for Jonathan, demonstrates grace to Jonathan's disabled son.* Likewise God—out of love for His Son, Jesus Christ, and through the penalty Christ paid on the cross for our sins—demonstrates grace to the believing sinner. God is still seeking people who are spiritually disabled, dead due to depravity, lost in trespasses and sins, hiding from God, broken, fearful, and confused. Those who walk with God today are doing so only because He demonstrated His grace to us out of love for His Son.

4. *Mephibosheth has nothing, deserves nothing, can repay nothing.* He makes no attempt to win the king's favor. He has been hiding from the king. The same is true of us. We deserve nothing, have nothing, and can offer God nothing. We were hiding when He found us.

5. *David restores Mephibosheth from a place of barrenness to a place of honor.* He takes this broken, handicapped person from a hiding place where there's no pastureland and brings him to the place of plenty within the king's palace. The analogy is clear. God has taken us from where we were and brought us to where *He* is—to a place of fellowship with Him. He has restored us to what we once had in Adam.

6. *David adopts Mephibosheth into his family, and he becomes one of the king's sons.* This is what God has done for the believing sinner—adopted us into the family of the heavenly King. He has chosen us, brought us into His family, and said, "Sit at My table, enjoy My food—I give you My life." Every Christian is adopted as a family member of God.

7. *Mephibosheth's disability is a constant reminder of grace.* He has nothing but crutches, yet he receives the bounty of the king. Every time he limps from room to room, from one step to the next, he's reminded: *I'm in this*

magnificent place, enjoying the pleasures of this position, only because of the grace of the king—and no other reason.

That's the way it is with the Father. Our continual problem with sin is a continual reminder of His grace. Every time we claim His promise of forgiveness, we remind ourselves that grace is available. That's when the Lord covers our feet with His tablecloth and says, "Have a seat. You're Mine. I chose you simply because I wanted to."

8. *When Mephibosheth sits down at the king's table, he's treated like a son of the king.* That's the way it is now, and the way it will be throughout eternity as we feast with our Lord—and, yes, with King David himself, along with Mephibosheth. And the Lord will look at each of us and say, "You're Mine. You're as important to Me as all my other sons and daughters. Here's the meal."

It will take eternity for us to adequately express how much this truth means to us.

Grace. It really is *amazing!*

———

GOING AFTER GOD'S OWN HEART: From David's Psalm 86, make his prayer your own:

> You, Lord, are a compassionate and gracious God,
> slow to anger, abounding in love and faithfulness.
> Turn to me and have mercy on me;
> show your strength in behalf of your servant. (86:15–16)

CHAPTER 16

A ROOFTOP CHOICE

The Bible never flatters its heroes. All the men and women in Scripture have feet of clay, and when the Holy Spirit paints a portrait of their lives, He's a realistic artist. He doesn't ignore, deny, or overlook the dark side.

No sin except the sin of Adam and Eve has received more press than the sin of David with Bathsheba. But it's good to remember that David is still a man after God's heart. He sins—but his sin is no greater than your sin or mine; it's just that ours haven't been recorded for everyone to read throughout the rest of history. Admittedly, David's sin is intensified because of who he is and how he mishandles it. But it's just sin—disobedience that he'll later come to regret with bitter tears.

You and I know such experiences, not in the same details as David but in the sorrowful aftermath.

I'm not justifying David's sin. And as you'll see, I'm certainly not defending it. I'm just trying to give proper perspective. If you cluck your tongue at David, you've completely missed the warning: "Let him who thinks he stands take heed lest he fall" (1 Corinthians 10:12 NKJV). Wedged between "stand" and "fall" in that verse are the words "take heed." We need to do that on a regular basis. If we don't take heed by running as fast as we can from this kind of temptation, *we will fall*, as surely as David does.

My point: David's flesh and our flesh are equally weak. Unless we stay alert and aware, our flesh will lead us into a similar sinful excursion, with consequences and grief just as bitter as his. With that in mind, let's see what we can learn from this man's tragic failure.

A DARK BACKDROP

David is now about fifty years old, perhaps a few years older. He's been on the throne approximately twenty years. He's distinguished himself as a man of God, a composer of psalms, a faithful shepherd, a valiant warrior on the battlefield, and a leader of his people. He has not only led the people in righteousness; he's also given them the glorious worship music of the Psalms. He's a man of passion as well as compassion. And we've seen him demonstrating grace and showing honor by taking in Mephibosheth, thus keeping his promise to Jonathan and to Saul.

So in this next season in David's life, we're not examining the life of a wild rebel or a sexual pervert. However, for a period of time he falls into sin, and it will have devastating consequences for his family, his reign, and his nation. *Sin always bears consequences.* That's why we're to take heed lest we fall, whatever our age. No one ever gets too old to fall.

At this point, David's life is like a neglected seawall standing against the barrage of the tide and waves of the ever-pounding sea—unguarded and in a weakened moment, it crumbles. And David will pay a terrible price.

He doesn't fall suddenly. In his spiritual armor, some chinks have already begun to form.

David clearly realizes his God-given privilege—that the hand of God has been on him, and the Lord's blessing has been abundant: "David knew that the LORD had established him as king over Israel and had exalted his kingdom for the sake of his people Israel" (2 Samuel 5:12).

But there are areas of private neglect that will take their toll: "After he left Hebron, *David took more concubines and wives* in Jerusalem, and more sons and daughters were born to him" (5:13). David has continued to increase the number of his wives and concubines—in direct contradiction to God's written commandments. In His laws given to Moses, we find clearly stated requirements for Israel's kings:

> When you enter the land the LORD your God is giving you and have taken possession of it and settled in it, and you say, "Let us set a king over us like all the nations around us," be sure to appoint over you a king the LORD your God chooses. . . . The king, moreover, must not acquire great

numbers of horses for himself. . . . *He must not take many wives,* or his heart will be led astray. He must not accumulate large amounts of silver and gold. (Deuteronomy 17:14–17)

God declared at least three things that the king of Israel must not do: multiply horses for himself, multiply his wives, and multiply his silver and gold. David has been faithful in the first and the third requirements; but being a man of passion, he fails in the second. And even as his wives and concubines increase, his passion isn't abated. This king, who'll soon take another man's wife, already has a harem full of women. Contrary to a lie that pervades our society today, the simple fact is that sexual passion isn't satisfied by sleeping with numerous women; it's *increased.* Having many women stimulates a man's libido, rather than reducing it. David, a man with a strong sexual appetite, finds that appetite only increasing.

And just who in the kingdom is qualified and ready to blow the whistle on David?

They look at his track record: A humble beginning. A giant-killer. Two decades of sterling leadership. Choice men placed in the right roles. A military force every foe respects. No defeats on the battlefield. National boundaries vastly enlarged. Exports, imports, and financial health. A beautiful new home, and plans for the temple of the Lord. Against such a king, who could point a finger of accusation? If he marries a few more women and privately increases the number of his concubines . . . well, so what?

So what? Well, first of all, the king's heart gets led astray from the Lord—exactly as the Lord warned about in Deuteronomy 17. Daniel's lust and polygamy have secretly begun to erode his integrity and his reverence for the Lord.

Second, his vulnerability is increased. Between chapters 5 and 11 in 2 Samuel, we see nothing but success for David. He's at an all-time high, fresh off a series of great battlefield victories. He reaches the peak of public admiration. He has ample money, incredible power, unquestioned authority, remarkable fame. The course of his life is like an arrow climbing higher and higher into the clouds. Therefore—he is now especially vulnerable.

Our most challenging times are not when life is difficult. Hard times create dependent people. You don't get proud when you're forced to depend on God. Survival keeps you humble. Pride happens when everything is swinging in your direction. When you've just received that promotion or raise, or you're growing in prestige and prominence and significance—that's the time to watch out, especially if you're unaccountable to others, as David is in his situation.

So he begins indulging himself. That's another chink in the armor—indulgence. We've seen already how David indulges his sons, leaving responsibility for his family to others while he engages in battle. And when the bills come due, he's too relaxed to face his responsibilities.

Now the sphere of indulgence widens.

A SENSUAL SCENE

At this point of vulnerability and indulgence in David's fiftieth year of life, we read this about him:

> In the spring, *at the time when kings go off to war*, David sent Joab out with the king's men and the whole Israelite army. They destroyed the Ammonites and besieged Rabbah. But *David remained in Jerusalem*.
> One evening *David got up from his bed* . . . (2 Samuel 11:1–2)

David is in bed, not in battle. Had he been where he belonged—with his troops—there would never have been the Bathsheba episode. Our greatest battles don't usually come when we're working hard; they come when we're at leisure, with time on our hands, when we're bored. That's when we make those fateful decisions that come back to haunt us.

The king is indulging himself beyond the boundaries of wisdom. He belongs in the battle; we find him instead in his bedchamber, perhaps an elegantly furnished room. David pushes back the bedspread, stretches himself, and sighs as he looks around him. Richly woven draperies billow beside the open windows, as warm breezes blow. It's a lovely springtime evening in Jerusalem; fading sunset rays still color the skies, where the first stars make their appearance.

He certainly isn't needing more sleep. What his body is feeling is not the exhaustion of a busy, productive man, but something else. *Perhaps I need a walk,* he thinks. Eastern monarchs frequently put their bedchambers on the second story of the palace, with a door opening onto what we might call a patio roof. This outdoor area was comfortably furnished, a private place to be with family or advisers, well apart from the streets below. That's where David goes on this unforgettable night.

"David . . . walked around on the roof of the palace" (11:2). His is a large home with plenty of space out there. Looking out from the roof's height, he takes in evening scenes and sights. Perhaps a faintly distant sound of splashing catches his attention; David turns and looks. "From the roof he saw a woman bathing. The woman was very beautiful" (11:2).

The Bible never pads the record. When the passage says that the bathing woman he observes is "very beautiful," we know she's physically attractive almost beyond description. David stares. He lusts. He will seek her. He has lost control of his passion.

In his book *Temptation*, Dietrich Bonhoeffer wisely strikes at the heart of the problem that you and I, like David, wrestle with:

> In our members there is a slumbering inclination toward desire, which is both sudden and fierce. With irresistible power, desire seizes mastery of the flesh. All at once a secret, smoldering fire is kindled. The flesh burns and is in flames. It makes no difference whether it is a sexual desire, or ambition, or vanity, or desire for revenge, or love of fame and power, or greed for money. . . .
>
> At this moment God is quite unreal to us. [Remember those words.] He loses all reality, and only desire for the creature is real. The only reality is the devil. Satan does not here fill us with hatred of God, but with forgetfulness of God. . . .
>
> It is here that everything within me rises up against the Word of God. . . . Therefore the Bible teaches us in times of temptation in the flesh, there is one command: Flee! Flee fornication. Flee idolatry. Flee youthful lusts. Flee the lusts of the world. There is no resistance to Satan in lust other than flight. Every struggle against lust in one's own strength is doomed to failure.[16]

If you don't run, you will fall. If you try to fight it, you'll fall. It's only a matter of time. Lust backs off only when you run from the temptation.

Standing on his palace roof in the evening air, with no one else around, David loses all cognizance of who he is or what will happen if he yields to his lust for this woman. As the smoldering desire within him bursts into flames, he forgets that he's God's man. God becomes quite distant and unreal to Israel's king.

Blinded by desire, he becomes engulfed with imagination. He wants this woman *now!* "David sent someone to find out about her. The man said, 'She is Bathsheba, the daughter of Eliam and the wife of Uriah the Hittite'" (11:3).

The wording of this report is significant. The soft-footed servant offers the king a subtle warning of wisdom. The woman is not only someone's daughter; she's someone's wife. This servant, it appears, knows exactly what David's thinking. The servant is an adult male as well, and he knows his master, and he has seen the harem. He has watched David operate with women. Hence the warning.

Which doesn't seem to register in the least with David. Out of control, he says no to what he should be saying yes to, and yes to what he should be saying no to. In this moment, God is unreal to David; the only reality is the desire for sexual pleasure with this woman.

David moves quickly: "Then David sent messengers to get her. She came to him, and he slept with her" (11:4).

Let's be absolutely realistic here. We would be foolish to think that there's no pleasure in this encounter between David and Bathsheba. This act carries with it enormous sensual excitement. Stolen waters *are* sweet. Both of them probably take thorough pleasure in this private moment. He's romantic and handsome; she's beautiful, flattered, and lonely (her husband is away on duty at the battlefield). Nothing in the passage indicates that David has to force himself upon this woman. It appears to be a consensual adulterous act, a one-time-only mutual situation that brings mutual satisfaction.

And we read, "Then she went back home" (11:4). Perhaps before midnight she's in her own chamber, hoping no one has noticed her evening out.

This man and woman on this spring night are able "to enjoy the fleeting pleasures of sin" (to borrow the phrase from Hebrews 11:25)—but the pleasure is indeed fleeting, gone within a matter of weeks: "The woman conceived and sent word to David, saying, 'I am pregnant'" (2 Samuel 11:5).

It's been my observation over the years that the devil never tips his hand in temptation. He shows you only the beauty, the ecstasy, the fun, the excitement, the stimulating adventure of stolen desires. He never tells the heavy drinker, "Tomorrow morning there'll be a hangover, and ultimately you'll ruin your family." He never tells the first-time drug user, "This is the beginning of a long, sorrowful, dead-end road." He never tells the thief, "You're going to get caught, and you'll wind up behind bars." He certainly doesn't warn the adulterer, "You know, pregnancy is a real possibility," or, "You could get a life-threatening disease." But when the sin is over and all its penalties come due, the devil is nowhere to be found. He smiles as you fall but leaves no encouragement when the consequences kick in.

F. B. Meyer succinctly stated the outcome for David:

> One brief spell of passionate indulgence, and then—his character blasted irretrievably; his peace vanished; the foundations of his kingdom imperiled; the Lord displeased; and great occasion given to his enemies to blaspheme![17]

A PANIC PLAN

"David, I'm pregnant." When the king gets this news, he has a decision to make. He can go before God and his family and nation and openly confess his guilt: "I have sinned." Or he can take the route of deception and hypocrisy.

Sadly, David chooses the latter, which leads him even further into sin—including the horrific act of murder. His choice sets in motion an endless series of heartaches within his immediate family for years to come. What a fool he is to try covering up his sin!

When we're in panic mode, we don't make wise decisions. And that's where David is. He has had his night of passion—so far as we know, he and Bathsheba have been together only that one evening. And suddenly the news jolts him: This woman carries *his* child, this woman who's another man's wife. *What do I do?*

He comes up with a creative idea: He'll hurry and get the woman's husband back from the battlefield and in bed with his wife. Yes, there's a pregnancy, but if Uriah sleeps with his wife, nobody will ever know David's part in it. "So David sent this word to Joab: 'Send me Uriah the Hittite.' And Joab sent him to David" (11:6).

The husband of beautiful Bathsheba now stands before his king: "When Uriah came to him, David asked him how Joab was, how the soldiers were, and how the war was going" (11:7). In this moment, did David really care about his soldiers or the state of the war or how well Joab was leading? Hardly. It's all talk, designed to make David look compassionate. He's merely setting up Uriah, putting him at ease.

> David said to Uriah, "Go down to your house and wash your feet." So Uriah left the palace, and a gift from the king was sent after him. (11:8)

It's a clever idea—and it flops. Uriah won't go home as David has commanded.

> But Uriah slept at the entrance to the palace with all his master's servants and did not go down to his house. (11:9)

When David learns of this, his deceitful scheme forces him to confront Uriah:

> He asked Uriah, "Haven't you just come from a military campaign? Why didn't you go home?"
> Uriah said to David, "The ark and Israel and Judah are staying in tents, and my commander Joab and my lord's men are camped in the open country. How could I go to my house to eat and drink and make love to my wife? As surely as you live, I will not do such a thing!" (11:10–11)

What a reproof to David! Uriah's a faithful soldier whose wartime heart is with the men in the field. While they're stuck at the front, Uriah doesn't dare seek the comfort of wife and home just for himself.

David—the commander in chief of these soldiers—should feel rebuked by this foot soldier's loyal commitment. But David is too insensitive to feel remorse. Look how he handles this:

> Then David said to him, "Stay here one more day, and tomorrow I will send you back." So Uriah remained in Jerusalem that day and the next. At David's invitation, he ate and drank with him, and David made him drunk.
>
> But in the evening Uriah went out to sleep on his mat among his master's servants; he did not go home. (11:12–13)

Uriah just will not cooperate.

David is likely frustrated to the point of rage over his failing plan. No matter what he tries, he can't pull off his strategy of deception. He can steal the man's wife, but he can't manipulate the woman's husband.

COVER-UP TO THE EXTREME

In greater panic, David escalates his plot to a far more despicable level.

> In the morning David wrote a letter to Joab and sent it with Uriah. In it he wrote, "Put Uriah out in front where the fighting is fiercest. Then withdraw from him so he will be struck down and die." (11:14–15)

David writes the message, seals it, and says, "Uriah, take this to Joab."

Let me ask you: Does David trust Uriah? All the way. He sends this loyal man off with his own death warrant in hand. And when Uriah reaches the battlefield and hands over the secure message to Joab, who then reads it—guess who puts two and two together?

As David's chosen military commander, Joab is a swift, clever, tough-minded warrior, excelling in battlefield leadership. (Even David is a little uneasy with this guy and the clout he carries.) Moreover, Joab is street smart—quick and bright. There's not a naive cell in Joab's body. In fact, I have a hunch he already has his suspicions, from back when he first got David's order to send Uriah home to Jerusalem. Joab, who of course knows Uriah well, probably also is aware of his beautiful wife.

Joab is no fool. He knows who he must please. And he knows exactly what's important to him.

Innocent Uriah is doomed.

> So while Joab had the city under siege, he put Uriah at a place where he knew the strongest defenders were. When the men of the city came out and fought against Joab, some of the men in David's army fell; moreover, Uriah the Hittite died.
>
> Joab sent David a full account of the battle. (11:16–18)

This battle account Joab composes shows just how well Joab understands what David really wants to hear:

> He instructed the messenger: "When you have finished giving the king this account of the battle, the king's anger may flare up, and he may ask you, 'Why did you get so close to the city to fight? Didn't you know they would shoot arrows from the wall? . . . Why did you get so close to the wall?' If he asks you this, then say to him, 'Moreover, your servant Uriah the Hittite is dead.'" (11:19–21)

Just let the king know: *Mission accomplished.*

The messenger from the battlefield reaches the king:

> When he arrived he told David everything Joab had sent him to say. . . . "The men overpowered us and came out against us in the open, but we drove them back to the entrance of the city gate. Then the archers shot arrows at your servants from the wall, and some of the king's men died. Moreover, your servant Uriah the Hittite is dead." (11:22–24)

Listening breathlessly, David finally hears what he's been waiting to hear: Uriah's dead. The king then adds an act of ultimate hypocrisy:

David told the messenger, "Say this to Joab: 'Don't let this upset you; the sword devours one as well as another. Press the attack against the city and destroy it.' Say this to encourage Joab." (11:25)

"Some of the king's men died," the messenger reports. It isn't just Uriah who falls in battle. Many on that battlefield pay the price for David's sin. Yet David can say, "Well, after all, that's war, you know—somebody always gets killed. But now, Joab, you know how to press this offensive in the right way; do it, and the victory's yours."

Rather than falling before God, declaring himself guilty of this crime, David moves right along. He knows what to do next to protect himself.

When Uriah's wife heard that her husband was dead, she mourned for him. After the time of mourning was over, David had her brought to his house, and she became his wife and bore him a son. (11:26–27)

When you act in panic, you don't think logically. In fact, you usually don't think. You react. You overlook and cover up and smear over and deny and scheme—until you find yourself in the midst of such a maze of lies, you can never escape it, or get the mess untangled.

Meanwhile, at the end of this shameful episode, we read these awful words: "But the thing that David had done was evil in the sight of the LORD" (11:27 NASB). David may be breathing a sigh of relief that all this is over—but the narrative's conclusion sends the signal that God is going to get the last word.

In 2 Samuel 11 we see the raw, open sewage of David's life. This exemplary leader is now shriveled into something he was never designed to be, because he deliberately compromised with immorality, then deceitfully covered it over with murder.

This story strikes some a lot harder than it does others. Some people live in the relentless rage of lust; they curse it, but it's there. They don't want it, but it constantly bites into them and paralyzes their spiritual walk, just as it does with David. I think God tells us these details of David's fall so we all can see clearly where it leads and what the consequences are.

Have you kept count of David's sins here? Lust, adultery, hypocrisy, murder. How could a man after God's own heart fall to such a level?

If you're honest about your own heart, it's not hard to understand.

If you're playing with sins of the flesh, you're living on borrowed time as a child of God. There's nothing more stinging and damning to life than hidden sins of the flesh. There's nothing that gives Satan greater ammunition for blasphemous statements about God and His church than this kind of secret compromise. And you can be part and parcel of it indirectly by not taking a stand against it.

And so, this sad, dark chapter of David's fall comes to an end.

Or does it?

Not really. David's now trapped in a swirl of misery, which he'll describe in detail in Psalms 32 and 51. Sleepless nights. Physical illness. Fever. Haunted memories. Total misery. What's worse, he feels terribly alone, so many miles from God. So full of groaning and agonizing. Read the opening verses of those psalms for yourself. Let them take shape in your mind. Don't hurry. We need to see afresh the wages of sin.

After many months have dragged on, a knock will come on the palace door, and a friend who cares enough to confront David will look him in the eye and call a spade a spade. It will be a visit David never forgets.

———

GOING AFTER GOD'S OWN HEART: From David's Psalm 139, make his prayer your own:

> You have searched me, LORD,
> and you know me. . . .
> If I say, "Surely the darkness will hide me
> and the light become night around me,"
> even the darkness will not be dark to you. (139:1,11–12)

CHAPTER 17

CONFRONTATION

For the better part of a year following his sins of adultery and murder, David's life is one of hypocrisy and deception. His world becomes one of guarded, miserable secrecy.

Looking back, and knowing of David's sins as we do, one might suppose that during these passing days and months, the holy God of heaven is asleep. Or at least, He's "letting it pass." One might think that sin actually *does* pay, that there are no wages for sin.

But that is not the case, then or now.

In a marvelous move on God's part, He finally brings before David a man of great integrity who tells him the truth. I don't think any confrontation has ever been so quickly effective as this one. Just a few simple words will cement the job: "You are the man!" Hearing that, David crumbles in humility. I suspect also that a fresh wave of relief comes over his soul.

Remember that David's sins, like many of our own, were carried out *secretly*—at least for a while. Individuals like David in positions of higher authority sometimes have power to give themselves increased privacy—which brings greater temptation for doing things in secret. Moreover, lack of accountability is also common among those in higher positions, leading to mistakes and moral lapses. So it is with David.

David's sins were also done *willfully*. These are not momentary mistakes. He doesn't stumble into them. He willfully and knowingly walks into adultery with Bathsheba, then arranges for the death of her husband—then deliberately lives a lie through the months that followed.

During those months, David's sins do not go unnoticed by God, as confirmed by that verse that summarizes the episode: "The thing that David had done was evil in the sight of the LORD" (2 Samuel 11:27 NASB). To those weighty words, I would add the following: "And don't you forget it!" What was evil three thousand years ago is evil today, no matter how many people do it. To cheapen a marriage with an adulterous relationship is still a willful sin, no matter how often it happens. This very night, in secret places, people with wedding rings given by another person will offer their bodies to individuals who are not their own partners. It's still evil in the sight of the Lord. Don't forget that.

Maybe nobody else notices what David has done and is doing, but God does. And He activates a strategy to bring the man to his knees. God is awfully good at that. He doesn't settle His accounts at the end of each month or each year. But when He does settle them—well, "Do not be deceived, God is not mocked," wrote the apostle Paul; "for whatever a person sows, this he [or she] will also reap" (Galatians 6:7 NASB).

As one of my mentors once put it, "God's wheels grind slowly, but they grind exceedingly fine."

WHAT THOSE MONTHS WERE LIKE

You may be thinking that David's life is enjoyable during these months of secrecy following his hidden sins—that David spends long, pleasureful nights free of guilt with his new wife. But we see something different in Psalms 32 and 51, which give David's retrospective take on those months. I briefly mentioned those psalms at the end of the last chapter. Let's look at them closely.

The title of Psalm 32 reads, "Of David. A maskil." The word *maskil* is taken from a Hebrew term that means "instruction." This is a psalm designed to instruct. Indeed it does!

It begins:

> Blessed is the one
> whose transgressions are forgiven,

whose sins are covered.
Blessed is the one
whose sin the LORD does not count against them
and in whose spirit is no deceit. (32:1–2)

Now listen to David's admission:

When I kept silent about my sin, my body wasted away
through my groaning all day long.
For day and night Your hand was heavy upon me;
my vitality failed as with the dry heat of summer.
(32:3–4 NASB)

The Living Bible paraphrases it well:

There was a time when I wouldn't admit what a sinner I was. But my dishonesty made me miserable and filled my days with frustration. All day and all night your hand was heavy on me. My strength evaporated like water on a sunny day.

In his splendid book *Guilt and Grace*, Paul Tournier, the brilliant Swiss writer, physician, and psychiatrist, talks about two kinds of guilt: true guilt and false guilt. False guilt, says Tournier, is brought on by the judgments and suggestions of man. True guilt comes from willfully and knowingly disobeying God.[18] Obviously, David is enduring true guilt.

To illustrate how people handle guilt differently, someone has mentioned the picture of the warning light on your car's dashboard. As you're driving along, the red light flashes—you're given notice that there's trouble under the hood. At that moment, you have a choice. You can stop, get out of the car, open the hood, and try to detect what's wrong. Or you can carry a small hammer with you, and when the red light appears, you can knock it out with the hammer and keep on driving. No one will know the difference—for a while, until you damage the engine. You'll then look back and realize what a stupid decision you made.

Some Christians carry imaginary hammers in their conscience. When the light of true guilt begins to flash, they bring out the hammer and knock out the light. *I shouldn't feel guilty; it's just what everybody else is doing*—and so on. But all the while their internal motor is getting damaged. Then, somewhere down the road, they realize how foolish it was to not stop and look deeper, and come to terms with what's wrong.

David acknowledges here his inward groaning. You know what that means. There's this awful oppression, this misery of conscience, day and night. What he feels is God's heavy hand upon him. It's like a fever. As his inner strength drains away, he can't adequately handle the pressures of his responsibilities.

In Psalm 51:3, David says, "I know my transgressions, and my sin is always before me"—he cannot get away from it. He can see it written across the ceiling of his bedroom as he tosses and turns on sleepless nights. He sees it on his plate while trying to choke down meals. He's a miserable husband, an irritable father, a poor leader, a songless composer. He's living a lie but cannot escape the truth.

Later in this psalm, David asks the Lord to restore his joy (51:12)—he has been living a joyless existence.

This psalm bears this title: "A Psalm of David. When the prophet Nathan came to him after David had committed adultery with Bathsheba." So David records these words after the fateful visit from Nathan—who stepped into David's life and told him the truth. Let's walk through this incredible confrontation.

A SUDDEN SWORD

It's worth noticing that Nathan doesn't come on his own; he's sent by God: "Then the LORD sent Nathan to David" (2 Samuel 12:1 NASB). Perhaps the most important word in that sentence is the first one: "Then . . ." God's timing is absolutely incredible.

When was Nathan sent? Right after the act of adultery? No. Is it right after Bathsheba said, "I am pregnant"? No. Right after David murdered Uriah? No. Right after he married Uriah's pregnant widow? No. Right after the birth of the baby? No. It's believed by some Old Testament scholars that at least twelve months pass after the adultery before Nathan pays this visit. God waits until just the right time. He lets the grinding wheels of sin do their full work upon David, and *then* He steps in.

To be fully honest, I sometimes question God's timing. I don't understand why He's so slow to carry out what I think He ought to do. But whenever I've looked back in retrospect, I've seen how beautifully He worked out His plan, how perfectly it came to pass. God not only does the right thing; He does the right thing at the right time.

In David's situation, God not only knows the right time; he also chooses the right person, a man who has earned David's respect over the years. Nathan the prophet needs no introduction; David knows him well.

Now put yourself in Nathan's sandals. Think of the difficult commission God has given him. Nathan is to stand before the most powerful man in the nation, and tell that man what he's refused to tell himself for a year.

No one else in the land has told David the truth. There may have been some raised eyebrows, some whispers. But nobody has been honest and forthright enough to say, "David, you're in sin."

So God sends Nathan to speak to David. And Nathan obeys immediately.

On his way to the palace, Nathan must be thinking through how he'll present this matter to David. After he's there, his opening words are both thoughtful and brilliant. With Nathan's story approach, David is drawn in and also disarmed of all defenses.

Nathan begins the story:

"There were two men in a certain town, one rich and the other poor. The rich man had a very large number of sheep and cattle, but the poor man had nothing except one little ewe lamb he had bought. He raised it, and it grew up with him and his children. It shared his food, drank from his cup and even slept in his arms. It was like a daughter to him." (12:1–3)

David listens attentively, perhaps recalling days in his youth as a shepherd when he himself held ewe lambs in his arms.

Nathan continues his wise words, as he puts David—unknowingly—in a vulnerable spot:

"Now a traveler came to the rich man, but the rich man refrained from taking one of his own sheep or cattle to prepare a meal for the traveler who had come to him. Instead, he took the ewe lamb that belonged to the poor man and prepared it for the one who had come to him." (12:4)

David's now on the edge of his chair. He's moved with empathy for the poor man, mixed with fierce indignation toward the rich man.

Then David's anger burned greatly against the man, and he said to Nathan, "As the LORD lives, the man who has done this certainly deserves to die! So he must make restitution for the lamb four times over, since he did this thing and had no compassion." (12:5–6 NASB)

With David's heated rush to judgment, he unwittingly sentences himself. The way is prepared. In that vulnerable, unguarded moment, David sticks his head in the noose. All Nathan has to do is give the rope a tug.

He does it in only two words in Hebrew (four in English): "*You* are the man!" (12:7).

The narrative doesn't say, but I'm convinced that David's jaw drops. As his own sins come silently and vividly to mind, he blinks and stares at Nathan. David wasn't aware that anyone fully knew what he'd done. Certainly he's never expected this trusted prophet to confront him about it.

But Nathan is the very best person to do it. "Faithful are the wounds of a friend" (Proverbs 27:6 NASB). More literally, the verse reads in Hebrew, "Trustworthy are the bruises caused by the wounding of one who loves you." Isn't that vivid? The one who loves you *bruises* you, and those lingering wounds are faithful, trustworthy. That kind of confrontation is the best thing in the world for any believer who's hiding secret sin. You're disarmed by the fact that your confronter is a friend (one who truly loves you)—and you melt like putty.

David's trusted friend and counselor is saying, "You, David, are the one who chose to take someone else's lamb, and satisfy your lust with her. David—*you are the man.*"

British biographer Alexander Whyte described the force of this confrontation in these words: "Nathan's sword was within an inch of David's conscience before David knew that Nathan had a sword. One sudden thrust, and the king was at Nathan's feet." And lest you and I get proudly judgmental toward David, Whyte added this: "Read Nathan's parable to yourself till you say, I am the man!"[19]

Before David can respond or interrupt, Nathan tells him more—which he prefaces with these words: "This is what the LORD, the God of Israel, says . . ." None of this is Nathan's message; it's *God's* message. The prophet is just the Lord's mouthpiece.

For David, here's the message from God at this time:

> "I anointed you king over Israel, and I delivered you from the hand of Saul. I gave your master's house to you, and your master's wives into your arms. I gave you all Israel and Judah. And if all this had been too little, I would have given you even more. Why did you despise the word of the LORD by doing what is evil in his eyes? You struck down Uriah the Hittite with the sword and took his wife to be your own. You killed him with the sword of the Ammonites. Now, therefore, the sword will never depart from your house, because you despised me and took the wife of Uriah the Hittite to be your own." (12:7–10)

In his sin, David has despised the God he serves, and he has despised His word. As a result, David in the coming days and years will experience piercing grief within his own household—a "sword" that will "never depart."

What a prediction! A quick look ahead in the biblical narrative reveals what this ever-thrusting sword means: turmoil and tragedy, rape and revenge, an uncontrollable son, another son who betrays him and drives his own father from the throne.

And just to be clear, Nathan declares again, "This is what the LORD says," as he delivers still more in this crushing message from God to David:

> "Out of your own household I am going to bring calamity on you. Before your very eyes I will take your wives and give them to one who is close to you, and he will sleep with your wives in broad daylight. You did it in secret, but I will do this thing in broad daylight before all Israel." (12:11–12)

Then silence fills the room. I can picture the king dropping to his knees as he gives the only appropriate response: "I have sinned against the LORD" (12:13).

With David's confession, his restoration begins.

Nathan immediately replies: "The LORD has taken away your sin. You are not going to die" (2 Samuel 12:13).

What a promise of grace! Though death for David would not be undeserved, this is not God's chosen punishment for him. However, Nathan then states the first of several harsh consequences: "Because by doing this you have shown utter contempt for the LORD, the son born to you will die" (12:14).

At this point, Nathan's mission is complete. End of confrontation. Nathan turns, walks out the door, and closes it—and the king is left alone. Perhaps it's that same evening when David writes Psalm 51. What relief forgiveness provides!

David can now tell himself, Finally, no more hiding. The truth is out. Finally, I have assurance of God's forgiveness. Finally, everything's out in the open before the Lord. It's like an infected sore being lanced so the pus can escape and healing can begin.

As we think seriously and personally about this moment in David's life, at least two lessons reach out for us. One has to do with effective confrontation; the other has to do with genuine repentance.

EFFECTIVE CONFRONTATION

If God calls you to be His messenger—as the friend who faithfully wounds a brother or sister in the Lord who has willfully stepped onto the wrong path—do it as skillfully and as humbly as Nathan did. Do it right, or don't do it. If God calls you to be a confronter, then confront. Call the sin what it is—certainly at the right time and in the right way, but do it! Don't hedge, don't try to redefine it, don't explain it away. Call it sin. And in doing so, remember that you, too, have sinned. Therefore stay humble and full of compassion. Speak the truth in love, yes—but *speak the truth!* Those who really care, care enough to confront.

People hunger for the message of God. A tremendous relief comes over the sinner to whom someone honestly says, "Face it, you've been wrong. Now do something about it."

To be effective in such confrontation, we need to equip ourselves with four things: absolute truth, right timing, wise wording, and fearless courage. Without these four, we can do more damage than good.

1. *Absolute truth*. Don't go on hearsay. Get the facts, which may take time. You may have to investigate. You do that out of love and concern. You uncover the facts and get them carefully recorded and correctly arranged. Without absolute truth, you're shooting in the dark.

2. *Right timing*. If we confront at the wrong time, this can drive the other person deeper into wrong. Wait until you're confident that it's God's timing. You will *know*—if you're sensitive to the Lord and are walking with Him. He will communicate to you, "Now is the time." Then you do it. And, like Nathan, you do it privately.

In my ministry, I've had to deal with some things that I would have preferred to deal with earlier. But it wasn't the time. When it finally was God's time, I had green lights flashing and knew the way was clear to speak to the person or persons involved. Painful, but clear.

3. *Wise wording*. I'm impressed that Nathan didn't just walk up to David and say, "You're in sin. I'm ashamed of you!" No, he went about it in a wise manner. He planned his approach carefully.

> A word fitly spoken is like apples of gold
> > in settings of silver.
> > Like an earring of gold and an ornament of fine gold
> > is a wise rebuker to an obedient ear. (Proverbs 25:11–12 NKJV)

Be wise in how you confront. The right words are crucial. If you don't have your wording worked out, don't go. Wait, and think it through.

4. *Fearless courage*. Nathan was sent by God—and that's where courage comes from. You'll have nothing to lose if you walk in the strength of the Lord. Don't fear the loss of a friendship. God honors the truth. After all, it's only the truth that sets people free. If the Lord is really in it, you'll be one of the best friends this person ever had by telling him the truth. Meanwhile, be certain that you're confronting out of love.

GENUINE REPENTANCE

An additional lesson we learn here is about genuine repentance itself. How can we know that repentance is genuine? I see four helpful guidelines in David's experience for identifying true repentance.

1. *When there's true repentance, there will be open, unguarded admission.* In Psalm 51, David tells the Lord, "Against you, you only, have I sinned and done what is evil in your sight" (51:4). He spells it out. When a person holds back the truth or tells you only part of it, he or she is not repentant.

2. *When there's true repentance, there's a desire to make a complete break from sin.* Repentance is turning around, on the basis of truth, and going in the opposite direction—making a complete break with what has been. "Whoever conceals their sins does not prosper, but the one who confesses and renounces them finds mercy" (Proverbs 28:13). Renouncing sin— forsaking sin—follows true confession of sin. The commitment is there to make a complete break.

3. *When there's true repentance, the spirit is broken and humble.* Again in his prayer in Psalm 51, David says, "My sacrifice, O God, is a broken spirit; a broken and contrite heart you, God, will not despise" (51:17). In genuine repentance, you won't be defensive or angry or proud or bitter. A contrite heart makes no demands and has no expectations. Broken and humble people are simply grateful to be alive. And from that broken and humble heart, emotions will overflow.

4. *True repentance is a claiming of God's forgiveness and reinstatement.* Turning around and going in the right direction is our claim that God has forgiven and reinstated us. That's the first thing Nathan does with his friend David: "You will not die, but there will be consequences." All sins are forgivable when confessed and forsaken, but some sins carry tremendous ramifications—the awful, sometimes lingering consequences. David will die hating the day he fell into bed with Bathsheba, because of the constant conflicts and consequences that resulted. But down inside he knows that the God of Israel has forgiven him and has dealt with him in *grace*. After all—he's allowed to go on living.

Of course, not all confrontations end like Nathan's experience with David. Sometimes, tragically, there's no repentance.

When we repent, God promises restitution and forgiveness through the blood of Jesus Christ. "If we confess our sins, he is faithful and just and will forgive us our sins and purify us from all unrighteousness" (1 John 1:9). He doesn't promise relief from any and all consequences, but He promises a relief that only the Holy Spirit of God can give.

The Spirit's work of purging is His most severe work. Our lives are either clean or dirty. Either we're keeping short accounts with our heavenly Father as His child, or we're living a lie—as David was, tragically, for so long.

GOING AFTER GOD'S OWN HEART: From David's Psalm 141, make his prayer your own:

> I call to you, LORD, come quickly to me;
> hear me when I call to you. . . .
> Let a righteous man strike me—that is a kindness;
> let him rebuke me—that is oil on my head.
> My head will not refuse it. (141:1,5)

CHAPTER 18

TROUBLE AT HOME

A family in trouble is a common occurrence, but it's never a pretty picture. The trouble can come from outside the family, or from within. Both can be devastating. But trouble from within is more difficult.

When your home burns to the ground, or a flood washes it off its foundation, the ensuing struggles are hard to bear. But I've found that those kinds of external troubles often pull a family together rather than apart.

Not so when troubles come from within—in the form of tension, abuse, neglect, unforgiveness, bitterness, heartbreaking hatred, and all the other difficulties that accompany the carnal life when parents walk in the flesh or act foolishly, or when children respond in rebellion and disagreement and disharmony. When there's friction between husband and wife or between parent and child, that's a lot harder to bear than external struggles. This is true especially when it's all about the consequence of someone's sin in the family.

Before we move on in David's life, I want to remind you again of a New Testament principle. It begins with the words "Do not be deceived"—words we read a number of times in the New Testament. The Lord gives us such warnings ahead of time because the devil or the flesh or the world will work havoc on our thinking, deceiving us into doubting the truth God presents. So God first says, "Don't be deceived about this. Don't let anyone teach you the opposite. Don't let yourself, or someone else, or some experience lead you to believe that something other than this is the truth."

So here again is the principle:

> Do not be deceived: God cannot be mocked. A man reaps what he sows.
> Whoever sows to please their flesh, from the flesh will reap destruction;
> whoever sows to please the Spirit, from the Spirit will reap eternal life.
> (Galatians 6:7–8)

We reap what we sow, forgiveness notwithstanding. If there's anything we've been duped into believing in our era of erroneous teachings on grace, it's the idea that if we simply confess our sins and claim God's forgiveness, it quickly eliminates all the consequences of what we've done.

But that's not what these verses (or any others in Scripture) say. Paul here was writing to people like you and me living in the era of grace. It's addressed to the church, to believers who are children of the King, who are in Christ, and living under grace.

Grace means that God, in forgiving you, does not kill you. Grace means that God, in forgiving you, gives you the strength to endure the consequences of your past sin. Grace frees us so that we can obey our Lord. It does not mean sin's consequences are automatically removed. If in anger I strike someone or something, and in the process I break my arm, then once I find forgiveness for that sin I still have to deal with the broken bone.

No one reading these words would deny that. We easily accept this principle in the physical realm. A broken arm is a broken arm, whether I've been forgiven or whether I'm still living under the guilt of my sin. But the same truth applies in the emotional life. When a parent willfully and irresponsibly acts against God's written Word, not only does the parent suffer, but the family suffers as well. And that means internal trouble that seriously affects other family members.

Look again at Paul's statement of cause and consequence: "Whoever sows to please their flesh, from the flesh will reap destruction." Our pleasure during the planting will be eclipsed by our pain in the harvest.

We're like farmers, walking through life, and as we walk along, we're planting one kind of seed or another every day. If we choose to sow the seeds of carnality, we may enjoy a measure of pleasure. Even Scripture declares that sin has its pleasures (short-lived though they are). That's what draws us into it. It's exciting, adventurous, stimulating. It satisfies the desires of the flesh. What we don't like to face, of course, is the pain that comes later.

Nothing concerns me more than today's propensity for using grace as a tool to justify sin or to take away the pain of the consequences. Too much teaching on corrective theology and not enough on preventive theology.

By way of example, think of what parents go through in teaching their teenager to drive. Parents of course have a choice in how to do this. They can teach them in a *corrective* manner or a *preventive* manner.

If we choose to teach correctively, we tell our teenager, "Now before we get in the car, I want to first of all show you the insurance policy I've taken out on this vehicle. So when you have a wreck, which you surely will, here's the phone number of our insurance agent. And here's the number of our local towing service. Oh, and be sure to call me." And we go into further detail about all the things to be done after a wreck. That would be a Corrective Driving Course.

On the other hand, we could tell our teenager, "If you drive by the rules and regulations and safety tips I'm going to teach you, and if you obey the roadside traffic signs, it's going to prevent a lot of problems ahead of time. You could very likely go a long period of time without even a slight scrape, though of course I can't guarantee it." That would be a Preventive Driving Course. I think you'd agree the preventive approach has the edge over the corrective.

Most of us were taught 1 John 1:9 long before we learned anything from Romans 6. Why? Because we've been trained to sin. Sounds heretical, doesn't it? But think about it. From the earliest days of our Christian life, we're taught this verse: "If we confess our sins, he is faithful and just and will forgive us our sins and purify us from all unrighteousness" (1 John 1:9). So when you sin, claim God's forgiveness. That's a marvelous verse. I call it our bar of soap in the Christian life. It keeps us clean. It certainly is the answer to the problem of sin, once sin has happened.

But it's not the *best* answer to the problem of sin. The best answer is found in Romans 6:

Therefore do not let sin reign in your mortal body so that you obey its evil desires. Do not offer any part of yourself to sin as an instrument of wickedness, but rather offer yourselves to God as those who have been brought from death to life; and offer every part of yourself to him as an instrument of righteousness. (6:12–13)

As we yield ourselves to God, when sin approaches, we can say no. In the power of Jesus Christ, we can turn away from win. We don't *have* to sin hour after hour, day after day.

Part of the reason we often don't catch the full truth of Romans 6 is that we talk too little about sin's consequences—which grace does not automatically take away.

If David could rise from the grave today, he would say "Amen" to that last statement. The sin in David's life led to trouble the likes of which few fathers on earth will ever experience.

Let's take a look at some of those downward steps that David's life takes, leading him to a life of misery as a result of his sin.

TROUBLE AT HOME

As we've seen, when Nathan confronts David with "You are the man," David admits: "I have sinned" (2 Samuel 12:7,13). Those three words are what he should have spoken the morning after he slept with Bathsheba. I'm convinced the consequences would have been far, far less if David had declared his sin back then, openly confessing it before God and the people, laying bare his error. But he didn't.

And now, a year later, Nathan tells David, "The sword will never depart from your house" (12:10).

Never?

Never.

"I thought David was forgiven," you say. Yes, he was. Nathan says so: "The Lord has taken away your sin. You are not going to die" (12:13). That's forgiveness. But there are still consequences—the promised sword.

Am I saying that everyone who sins will have the same consequences? No. God, in His sovereign and righteous way, fits the consequence to the person. It's His choice, His move, His plan. We don't know why He chooses to send one thing to some and something else to another. But in David's case, we know that He leads the king down a path of misery so that he'll never forget (nor will we, in retrospect) the consequences of that series of terrible choices on David's part.

In the Lord's message of coming punishment, mention is made twice of David's own house:

> "The sword will never depart from your *house*. . . . Out of your own *household* I am going to bring calamity on you." (12:10–11)

Other translations express that last verse this way: "I am raising up trouble against you from within your own family" (MLB); "I will cause your own household to rebel against you" (NLT); "I will raise up adversity against you from your own house" (NKJV). David will have to live under a constant threat from all those closest to him.

David has been forgiven, but his problems aren't over. For David and his family, the trouble comes from within—and I don't think words can express the awful pain this man experiences as he sees the misery unfold.

Many years ago, in his book *Down to Earth: The Laws of the Harvest*, my friend John W. Lawrence wrote this:

> When David sowed to the flesh, he reaped what the flesh produced. Moreover, he reaped the consequences of his actions even though he had confessed his sin and been forgiven for it. Underline it, star it, mark it deeply upon your conscious mind: *Confession and forgiveness in no way stop the harvest.* He [David] had sown; he was to reap. Forgiven he was, but the consequences continued. . . . What we sow we will reap, and there are *no exceptions.*[20]

Do you see what faulty theology has led us to believe? We've set ourselves up with a sin mindset. We've told ourselves that grace means all consequences of sin are instantly removed, so we let ourselves be sucked under by the power of the flesh rather than believing what Scripture teaches: *We don't have to sin* day after day after day. We sin only because we want to. We have the power in the person of the Holy Spirit to say no to it at every turn in our life. If we instead choose to say yes to sin, against the prompting of the Holy Spirit, we can be certain to end up in the backwash of the consequences. Unfortunately, so will innocent people closely related to us. Those domestic consequences are what create dysfunctional families.

DOWNWARD STEPS

In the downward trend in David's life, we now see compounding consequences that deepen David's misery.

The first family consequence is the loss of a child—the very child conceived in David's adultery. "The LORD struck the child that Uriah's wife had borne to David, and he became ill. . . . On the seventh day the child died" (12:15,18).

This, of course, brings grief to both David and Bathsheba, but in itself there's nothing shameful about it. That isn't the case with a host of other consequences. One particularly disgusting incident, with catapulting repercussions, is the rape of David's daughter by her half brother.

As we've seen, David's relations with his many wives and concubines have produced numerous children for him. Among them are Absalom and Tamar, a son and daughter who share the same mother, and son Amnon from a different mother.

Amnon is attracted to his half sister Tamar, who's described in 2 Samuel 13:1 as being beautiful. That attraction becomes uncontrolled lust:

> Amnon became so obsessed with his sister Tamar that he made himself
> ill. She was a virgin, and it seemed impossible for him to do anything to
> her. (13:2)

With the help of a friend, Amnon sets up a ruse. He lies in bed and fakes illness, then asks that his half sister be summoned to bring him food. Tamar complies.

> But when she took it to him to eat, he grabbed her and said, "Come to
> bed with me, my sister."

"No, my brother!" she said to him. "Don't force me! Such a thing should not be done in Israel! Don't do this wicked thing. . . ."

But he refused to listen to her, and since he was stronger than she, he raped her.

Then Amnon hated her with intense hatred. In fact, he hated her more than he had loved her. Amnon said to her, "Get up and get out!" (13:11–15)

In embarrassment and disgrace, Tamar goes to her brother Absalom, who keeps her under his protection.

And Absalom never said a word to Amnon, either good or bad; he hated Amnon because he had disgraced his sister Tamar. (13:22)

Lust has led to rape; rape has led to hatred. Now hatred leads to the next step, murder.

And where's David during all this? His daughter has been sexually violated by his son, and we read: "When King David heard all this, he was furious" (13:21); he was "very angry" (13:21 NASB). That's all! We hear of nothing else done or said. Classic passivity. Incredible paternal preoccupation. David's head is somewhere else.

These sons and daughters seem to have raised themselves, without proper parental authority and discipline—another consequence of sin in David's life.

What kind of palace has David provided physically for his umpteen wives and children? In appearances, it's no doubt fabulous. These women and children probably have every material thing they could want. But money can't buy the best things in life, or solve relationship problems within a home.

What a nightmare of a home this royal palace must be! No one has done a better job of describing it than Alexander Whyte, as he considered in particular Absalom's background:

Polygamy is just Greek for a dunghill. David trampled down the first and the best law of nature in his palace in Jerusalem, and for his trouble he spent all his after-days in a hell upon earth. David's palace was a perfect pandemonium of suspicion, and intrigue, and jealousy, and hatred—all breaking out, now into incest and now into murder. And it was in such a household, if such a cesspool could be called a household, that Absalom, David's third son by his third living wife, was born and brought up. . . .

A little ring of jealous and scheming parasites, all hateful and hating one another, collected round each one of David's wives. And it was in one of the worst of those wicked little rings that Absalom grew up and got his education.[21]

Absalom and his half brother Amnon do not speak for two full years, while bitterness and hatred eat away at Absalom. Finally, after patiently waiting for the right opportunity to exact his revenge, Absalom carries out a deceptive plan. He suggests that all the king's sons come together for a celebration at sheep-shearing time (a traditional time for festivities). Absalom invites his father, who declines the invitation:

"No, my son," the king replied. "All of us should not go; we would only be a burden to you." Although Absalom urged him, he still refused to go but gave him his blessing.

Then Absalom said, "If not, please let my brother Amnon come with us."

The king asked him, "Why should he go with you?" (13:25–26)

Now if David were on top of things in his own household, he'd be aware of the long-brewing hatred between these two brothers. There were questions to ask here, facts to uncover. David, however, falls prey to the wiles of his charming and handsome son: "But Absalom urged him, so he sent with him Amnon and the rest of the king's sons" (13:27).

Absalom "urged him"—meaning he badgers him, begs him, wheedles him. David's children manipulate him. And look what happens when all these sons get together:

Absalom ordered his men, "Listen! When Amnon is in high spirits from drinking wine and I say to you, 'Strike Amnon down,' then kill him. Don't be afraid. Haven't I given you this order? Be strong and brave."

So Absalom's men did to Amnon what Absalom had ordered.

Then all the king's sons got up, mounted their mules and fled. (13:28–29)

David will groan under the ache of it all: "The king's sons came in, wailing loudly. The king, too, and all his attendants wept very bitterly" (13:36).

In this continuing downward spiral, we move on now to a son's conspiracy and rebellion: "Meanwhile, Absalom had fled. . . . Absalom fled and went to Geshur," where his mother's father lived, and Absalom "stayed there three years" (13:34,38).

Finally, David's military commander Joab brings Absalom back to Jerusalem:

But the king said, "He must go to his own house; he must not see my face." So Absalom went to his own house and did not see the face of the king. . . . Absalom lived two years in Jerusalem without seeing the king's face. (14:24,28)

Finally, under Joab's persistent influence, father and son are reunited: "The king summoned Absalom, and he came in and bowed down with his face to the ground before the king. And the king kissed Absalom" (14:33).

However, behind the king's back, Absalom begins to steal the hearts of the people. He stands at the city gate, and as people come to seek David's counsel, Absalom intercepts them. He hugs and kisses them and wins their affection, as he questions and criticizes his father's leadership.

Before long, Absalom knows he has Israel's majority behind him.

Then Absalom sent secret messengers throughout the tribes of Israel to say, "As soon as you hear the sound of the trumpets, then say, 'Absalom is king. . . .'" And so the conspiracy gained strength, and Absalom's following kept on increasing. (15:10–12)

With all this momentum behind Absalom's maneuvering, the crisis for his father reaches the breaking point:

A messenger came and told David, "The hearts of the people of Israel are with Absalom."

Then David said to all his officials who were with him in Jerusalem, "Come! We must flee, or none of us will escape from Absalom. We must leave immediately, or he will move quickly to overtake us and bring ruin on us and put the city to the sword." (15:13–14)

David flees Jerusalem! And Absalom occupies the city and takes over the royal palace.

You'll recall that through the prophet Nathan, God has told David that He will take his wives "and give them to one who is close to you, and he will sleep with your wives in broad daylight . . . before all Israel" (12:11–12). That's exactly what happens now in Jerusalem, where the one "close" to David is his own son Absalom.

An adviser tells Absalom: "Sleep with your father's concubines whom he left to take care of the palace. Then all Israel will hear that you have made yourself obnoxious to your father" (16:21). Absalom agrees—and goes a step further. Notice where the act occurs: "They pitched a tent for Absalom on the roof, and he slept with his father's concubines in the sight of all Israel" (16:22). The palace roof is where David first fell into his sin leading to adultery and murder. Absalom's shameful display in that location is his way of telling David, "I'll rub your nose in it."

Absalom has built up his army, and they soon pursue David. But David has spies in Jerusalem who alert him about Absalom's specific plans, so David and his followers evade the attack. David has plenty of soldiers still loyal to himself; he skillfully organizes them in three groups and prepares them for battle with Absalom's forces. When the battle finally comes—in a dense forest—Absalom's troops are routed by David's army, at great cost:

The casualties that day were great—twenty thousand men. The battle spread out over the whole countryside, and the forest swallowed up more men that day than the sword. (18:7–8).

In the depths of that forest, where Absalom is trapped, David's commander Joab plunges three javelins into the heart of the king's son.

David meanwhile is awaiting word of the battle's outcome. Finally two runners come from the battlefield. The first cries out "All is well!"

> He bowed down before the king with his face to the ground and said, "Praise be to the LORD your God! He has delivered up those who lifted their hands against my lord the king." (18:28)

Immediately David asks, "Is the young man Absalom safe?" (18:29). He has earlier (in 18:5) cautioned all three of his commanders: "Be gentle with the young man Absalom for my sake" (words which Joab will brazenly ignore). David hopes to be reunited again with his son—whom he has never stopped loving, despite their long periods of estrangement.

But the first runner doesn't answer the king's question; he can only say that there was lots of confusion on the battlefield.

The second runner is a Cushite. He arrives and repeats the report given by the first runner.

> The king asked the Cushite, "Is the young man Absalom safe?"
> The Cushite replied, "May the enemies of my lord the king and all who rise up to harm you be like that young man." (18:32)

Which is the Cushite's way of saying, "Your son is dead."

What follows is probably the most grievous and pitiable parental scene in the Old Testament.

> The king was shaken. He went up to the room over the gateway and wept. As he went, he said: "O my son Absalom! My son, my son Absalom! If only I had died instead of you—O Absalom, my son, my son!" (18:33)

His grief persists, overwhelming him even as all his loyal troops return from their hard-fought victory. It's as if he doesn't see them or even think of them: "The king covered his face and cried aloud, 'O my son Absalom! O Absalom, my son, my son!'" (19:4).

David is a beaten man. He's strung out, sobbing as if he's lost his mind.

The death of Absalom is yet another step in this endless chain of devastating consequences—rape, hatred, murder, conspiracy, rebellion, death, and more death. The sword doesn't depart from David's house.

Surely David regrets the day he ever even looked at Bathsheba from that rooftop. The harvesting of his sins is almost more than he can bear.

GRACE TO FACE THE CONSEQUENCES

Hear it again, and welcome this graciously honest warning: "Do not be deceived: God cannot be mocked. A man [or woman] reaps what he [or she] sows" (Galatians 6:7).

If you've taken lightly the grace of God, if you've tiptoed through the corridors of God's kingdom, picking and choosing sin or righteousness at will, thinking that grace covers it all—you've missed it, my friend. You've missed it by a mile. As a matter of fact, it's quite likely that you're harvesting the bitter consequences of the seeds of sin planted in the past. Perhaps right now you're living in a compromising situation, or right on the edge of one. You're skimming along the surface, hoping it'll never catch up. But trust me: It will. God is not mocked.

Reality is that "the wages of sin is death" (Romans 6:23); reality also (from the rest of that verse) is this: "but the gift of God is eternal life in Christ Jesus our Lord."

Turn to Him right now. Turn your life over to Him. Broken and bruised and twisted and confused, just lay it all out before Him. Ask Him to give you the grace and strength to face the consequences realistically and straight on.

A number of years ago, I counseled a young man not yet twenty who'd been sent to me by his parents in hopes I might "talk some sense into his head" (their words).

With a curled lip and a grim face, he sat alone with me in my office, staring coldly at me as we talked. He was angry—bitter to the core. Obviously, he had deep wounds.

I said to him, "Tell me about your dad."

He uttered an oath and cleared his throat as he turned and looked out the window. "My dad! My one great goal is to kill him." His voice trailed off as he added, "I tried once and I failed, but next time I won't . . ."

He went on, seething with emotion, to describe time after time when his father had ridiculed him, embarrassed him, even beaten him. Now he was taller than his dad, and it was just a matter of time till he got even.

A chill ran up my spine as I listened to this modern-day Absalom vent his spleen. The more we talked, the clearer it became: This young man was the product of a tragic set of circumstances in a home that most people, from outward appearances, would consider Christian. Deep within those private relationships were all the marks of sinful habits: parental neglect, abusive behavior, unresolved conflict, and the lack of honesty, forgiveness, understanding, and (most of all) genuine love. The father, not unlike David, was well-respected in the community and among his professional peers. No one would have guessed there was such trouble at home, unless they got close enough to that son to see the scars. I've often wondered whatever became of that young man.

To everyone else, David was king. To Absalom, David was Dad. I wonder how Absalom would describe David, if he, being dead, could speak?

GOING AFTER GOD'S OWN HEART: From David's Psalm 51, make his prayer your own:

> Have mercy on me, O God,
> according to your steadfast love;
> according to your abundant mercy
> blot out my transgressions. . . .
> Behold, you delight in truth in the inward being,
> and you teach me wisdom in the secret heart. (51:1,6 ESV)

CHAPTER 19

RIDING OUT THE STORM

Some of the most difficult experiences for the Christian emerge in the backwash of sin. This is something we don't like to think or talk about within the family of God, but it needs to be addressed. And, in fact, it might surprise you to know how often God's Word addresses it.

Back in the Old Testament, tucked away in the writings of the prophet Hosea, is a verse I mentioned briefly in an earlier chapter. Announcing a stern message from God to Israel, His rebellious people, Hosea wrote, "They sow the wind and reap the whirlwind" (8:7). The prophet was describing the nation of Israel. They had cried out to God as if they knew Him, this nation that "set up kings without my consent," said the Lord (8:4). This nation walked in their own way (sowing the wind), and they suffered the consequences (reaping the whirlwind). It's the same principle we've observed in Paul the apostle's New Testament teaching: "The one who sows to his own flesh will reap destruction from the flesh" (Galatians 6:8 NASB).

David's life has reached a similar impasse. God loves him deeply, so He disciplines him severely. David needs to learn to *take God seriously*. God means what He says about holiness, both His and ours: "Just as he who called you is holy, so be holy in all you do" (1 Peter 1:15). When we choose willfully and deliberately to disobey our holy God, He doesn't wink at our sin and cover it over lightly, as if His grace lets Him overlook disobedience. Grace assures us that He won't kill us. Grace is our help during the time of the whirlwind, holding us together, keeping us strong, stabilizing us. But we may be sure that whatever breezy sinful seeds we drop in the ground, we'll reap the harvest of sin's whirlwind. By God's grace we'll survive as we ride out the storm—but the pain will at times seem unbearable.

Some of the suffering we experience in life is what we *deserve* because of our sinful disobedience; but there's also suffering we don't deserve, which we experience in the backwash of someone else's transgression. How tragic when innocent bystanders get caught in that! So how do we ride out a storm caused by either our own sin or another's—when we're reaping either our own whirlwind or someone else's? How do we handle it? The best illustration of this in Scripture is found in the life of David.

FACING THE TRUTH

Let's go back to Nathan's confrontation with this man. Without reservation or rationalization, David has confessed his guilt for adultery and murder: "I have sinned against the LORD." And Nathan responds, "The LORD has taken away your sin. *You are not going to die*" (2 Samuel 12:13). There's the promise of amazing grace! Under Old Testament law, adulterers were to be stoned and murderers executed—no exceptions. "Show no pity: life for life, eye for eye, tooth for tooth" (Deuteronomy 19:21). Grace at this moment came to David's rescue. His life was spared.

You'll recall that as Nathan gives God's message to David, he adds: "Because by doing this you have shown utter contempt for the LORD, the son born to you will die" (2 Samuel 12:14). What awful news for David to hear! And it's only the first in a series of dreadful consequences announced for him—tragic results serving as a permanent reminder that one who sows the wind will reap the whirlwind; one who sows to the flesh will reap corruption. So what can we learn from David about weathering the hardships?

A RIGHTEOUS RESPONSE

In David's life I find many helpful guidelines for navigating such storms. First: David's initial response was *prayer.* When his and Bathsheba's child became ill, "David pleaded with God for the child. He fasted and spent the nights lying in sackcloth on the ground" (12:16).

Today we know too little of that kind of protracted prayer and fasting. More often than not our response to sin is rather glib. We say, "Well, Lord, I've blown it again. And now I agree with You that the blood of Jesus Christ cleanses me from all sin. Thank You." And we go right on with our lives, until—"Oops, blew it again. Sorry, Lord."

That's not how David responded. When the promised whirlwind began, when he felt the hot winds of judgment begin to blow upon him, he fell before God and lay on the ground all night, repeatedly. He fasted, he waited on the Lord, he sought the Lord's mercy. He "pleaded with God for the child." He hoped for additional favor and grace. Undeserving though he was, he knew that his God of steadfast love was full of mercy and grace. David made no demands—but he implored God to spare the baby's life.

I can imagine the passionate words of prayer arising from David's heart on those sleepless nights: "Lord, I call upon You and upon Your grace. I ask You to alter Your plan, if that is possible. I plead with You to keep this son of ours alive. I don't deserve that gift, nor have I in any way earned the right to even make so bold a request. But I ask You to be merciful. I ask this of You because it's the sincere and humble desire of my heart. I have heard what You have said, and I will accept what You send. But I ask, I entreat You: Is it possible that You can give us this child?"

David prayed with a contrite heart, not letting himself be sidetracked from this solitude before God. "The elders of his household stood beside him to get him up from the ground, but he refused, and he would not eat any food with them" (12:17).

David apparently doesn't leave the house during this ordeal, or go to the place of worship. (We know this because later, after the child's death, we read that he washes and changes his clothes before going to the house of the Lord, where he worships.) David also doesn't go out and talk about what he's going through, making it everyone's business.

We learn from this that when we go through deep distress—whether brought on by our own sinfulness or someone else's—it's wise and biblical to pursue solitude. Sometimes we don't need to surround ourselves with people, no matter how well-meaning they are. Solitude is essential. Stay in the Lord's presence and seek His mind during this painful time.

There's nothing wrong with being alone for soul-searching times. These are moments when we're guided by this precept: "Watch over your heart with all diligence, for from it flow the springs of life" (Proverbs 4:23 NASB). Some things are too precious to share with others—too deep, too personal, too painful, too profound. In the soul-searching of our lives, we're to stay quiet so we can hear God say all that He wants to say to us in our hearts.

David prayed—and so must we. In his case, he stayed at it for seven full days, virtually uninterrupted.

David's further response also includes *facing the consequences realistically*.

On the seventh day the child died. David's attendants were afraid to tell him that the child was dead, for they thought, "While the child was still living, he wouldn't listen to us when we spoke to him. How can we now tell him the child is dead? He may do something desperate." (2 Samuel 12:18)

David's servants seem afraid that he might even commit suicide if they announce his son's death. They've been regarding his soul-searching solitude as deep and dangerous depression. But his realistic response is a far cry from anything suicidal:

David noticed that his attendants were whispering among themselves, and he realized the child was dead. "Is the child dead?" he asked.

"Yes," they replied, "he is dead."

Then David got up from the ground. After he had washed, put on lotions and changed his clothes, he went into the house of the LORD and worshiped. Then he went to his own house, and at his request they served him food, and he ate. (12:19–20)

David has spent seven days on his face alone before his Lord—inquiring of God, waiting and wondering if He in grace might spare the child. He's placed himself at God's disposal, abandoning himself in total seclusion. Then he hears those words: "Yes, the child is dead." He quietly gets up, takes a bath, changes his clothes, goes to the house of God—and *worships*. Which reminds me of Job, after experiencing tragic loss:

He fell to the ground in worship and said:

"Naked I came from my mother's womb,
and naked I will depart.
The LORD gave and the LORD has taken away;
may the name of the LORD be praised." (Job 1:20–21)

When you face the consequences of the whirlwind, you must guard against bitterness. Due to the pain that comes your way—especially since you've already confessed your sins to the Lord and agonized over how wrong you were—you'll have to guard against blaming God, because counter thoughts will invade: *How could You do this to me, Lord? I've served You these many years, and now look what You've taken from me!*

There's none of that in David's response. He immediately accepts what has happened, then he worships the Lord. This is a good time to remind ourselves that David is still a man after God's own heart.

Many would gasp in amazement at David's response. His child has just died; God's answer to his seven-day prayer has been a firm no. David's response seems to say, "What God has done, I accept from Him without hesitation—and *I will go on from here.*" It's an incredibly mature response, difficult though that may be for some to understand. But a contrite heart makes no demands and clings to no expectations.

David's response also includes *claiming the truth of Scripture.* David settles his case with God by resting in the truth of His Word. When crisis strikes is always the time to dive into Scripture on your own. Don't let your emotions be your guide or you'll do something rash or foolish. There's no counsel like God's counsel, no comfort like His comfort, no wisdom more profound than that revealed in His Word!

Others are often amazed when our response to hardship isn't "normal" (their word). They expect us to fall apart, to lose it. When David's servants can't understand his reaction to the news of his son's death, they ask him, "Why are you acting this way? While the child was alive, you fasted and wept, but now that the child is dead, you get up and eat!" (2 Samuel 12:21). Look at how David answers:

> "While the child was still alive, I fasted and wept. I thought, 'Who knows? The LORD may be gracious to me and let the child live.' But now that he is dead, why should I go on fasting? Can I bring him back again? *I will go to him*, but he will not return to me." (12:22–23)

David's response is one of the few passages in the Scriptures that help us know the eternal destiny of small children and infants who die. David affirms, "I'll go to him, but he won't return to me." That's a statement based on solid theology. From what David has learned about the Lord's love and power and eternal sovereignty as revealed in Old Testament law and history—as well as, for us, in the New Testament—he has faith in being reunited with this child in eternity. David faces the fact of this child's departure from this world. He accepts it; he doesn't deny it.

When we face a loved one's death, we, too, can rely on the comfort and counsel of God's Word to get through this crisis of grief. We know we can't bring our loved one back; we don't deny this or try to bargain with God about it. If you've lost an infant, this verse teaches that you cannot bring the child back, but you *will* see that child in heaven. You'll see that gift from God that He gave you and then took from you, for reasons known only to Him. After claiming this truth of Scripture, the stability you'll experience will amaze you.

Which leads to another response from David: *He refuses to give up.* When suffering the backwash of sin, our tendency can be to say, "I'm through. I'm finished with life. It isn't worth it any longer." But look at what David does:

> Then David comforted his wife Bathsheba, and he went to her and made love to her. She gave birth to a son, and they named him Solomon. The LORD loved him; and because the LORD loved him, he sent word through Nathan the prophet to name him Jedidiah. (12:24–25)

David comforts his wife. Don't forget that she also is grieving. Both of them are experiencing grief. They weep, then they go on living.

David is once more walking with the Lord as he did in days past.

One of the most pathetic scenes on earth is a child of God who sits in the corner too long, licking his wounds in self-pity. It takes spiritual strength and purpose to recover and move on after a crisis. "I'll go on, I'll pick up the pieces, I'll get back on target, back to work, back to living. I'll enjoy my friends again. I'll carry on as I did before. And by God's grace, I'll be wiser and more effective than I was before."

PLACE OF LONELINESS

What's it like to ride out the storm? What have we learned from David?

1. Riding out the storm is a *lonely* experience. You'll never be more alone emotionally than when you are in the whirlwind of consequences. You'll wish others could help you, but they can't. They'll want to be there, they'll care—but for the most part, you have to ride out the storm alone.

2. Riding out the storm is also a *learning* experience. In Psalm 32—a psalm that recounts David's misery during his months of secrecy and hypocrisy—he also imparts these words of ministry and encouragement:

> I will instruct you and teach you in the way you should go;
> I will counsel you with my loving eye on you.
> Do not be like the horse or the mule,
> which have no understanding
> but must be controlled by bit and bridle
> or they will not come to you.
> Many are the woes of the wicked,
> but the LORD's unfailing love
> surrounds the one who trusts in him. (32:8–10)

3. Riding out the storm, thank God, is also a *temporary* experience. It may be the most difficult time in your life, and it may seem that it will never end. But believe me, the whirlwind is temporary. Your faithful, caring Lord will see you through it.

My wife Cynthia and I have sometimes had to ride out a storm that seemed too painful to endure, while suffering under the consequences of another's disobedience. So my words in this chapter are anything but theoretical. We've identified with David's loneliness and solitude—his pleadings for grace, his protracted prayers mixed with fasting, his sincere desire for mercy. We've known, firsthand, whereof David speaks. Our waiting and weeping continued while the storm went on, as we waited and continued to wait. But by faith, we have learned to claim His peace. Because of grace, we have known His mercy, even when our hearts remained broken and our eyes were never far from tears. And God has seen us through.

4. Finally, riding out the storm is a *humbling* experience. Here's a verse my wife and I frequently quote in times of testing; it's taken from words spoken to the people of Israel:

> You shall remember all the way which the LORD your God has led you
> in the wilderness these forty years, in order to humble you, putting you
> to the test, to know what was in your heart, whether you would keep His
> commandments or not. (Deuteronomy 8:2 NASB)

For the Israelites, their time in the wilderness was a whirlwind in which they learned to take God seriously, and that He means what He says. That's His intention also for our own experiences of whirlwind and wilderness.

GOING AFTER GOD'S OWN HEART: From David's Psalm 56, make his prayer to the Lord your own:

> I will present my thank offerings to you.
> For you have delivered me from death
> and my feet from stumbling,
> that I may walk before God
> in the light of life. (56:12–13)

CHAPTER 20

FRIENDS IN NEED

The poet Samuel Taylor Coleridge once described friendship as "a sheltering tree."[22] What a beautiful description of that special relationship! Reading those words, I think of my friends as great leafy trees spreading themselves over me, providing shade from the sun, and whose presence is a stand against the blast of winter's wind of loneliness. A great, sheltering tree; that's a friend.

For years, in one particular church I attended as a young man, I was taught that if you're really mature, you don't need anybody else—that it's only the weak person who needs others. How wrong that teaching was! Even Jesus our Lord had many friends around Him during His earthly sojourn, and at least three of those friends were particularly intimate. If having friends is a sign of immaturity, why did Jesus have so many?

The truth of the matter is this: It is *not* a sign of weakness and immaturity to have a friend, or to need a friend. It's a sign of immaturity to think you *don't* need a friend.

ONE BROKEN MAN

In the next stage of David's life, we find a man who has a whole grove of sheltering trees—all much needed.

Let's review David's situation.

Personally, he is awash in guilt over his adultery with Bathsheba and his murder of her husband, and over living so many months afterward like a hypocrite. He has been eaten up with guilt, as Psalms 32 and 51 confirm.

Domestically, his home is shattered. He has lost a child and is watching his family crumble. As we've seen, his now-grown children experience incest, rape, anger, bitterness, murder, and rebellion, culminating in the conspiracy against him led by his cherished son Absalom. Is there any pain worse than family troubles?

Politically, David is losing respect and authority as a leader. He has a growing number of critics. They see that their hero has feet of clay.

So David is hurting—personally, domestically, and politically. As we've seen earlier, it's at this point that Absalom's conspiracy blossoms. Let's look closer at what that was all about.

> In the course of time, Absalom provided himself with a chariot and horses and with fifty men to run ahead of him. He would get up early and stand by the side of the road leading to the city gate. Whenever anyone came with a complaint to be placed before the king for a decision, Absalom would call out to him, "What town are you from?"
>
> He would answer, "Your servant is from one of the tribes of Israel."
>
> Then Absalom would say to him, "Look, your claims are valid and proper, but there is no representative of the king to hear you." And Absalom would add, "If only I were appointed judge in the land! Then everyone who has a complaint or case could come to me and I would see that they receive justice." (2 Samuel 15:1–4)

Sounds like Absalom's running for office, doesn't it? And that's exactly what he's doing without saying so. His technique is based on lies and treachery. When people come to the king to settle complaints or seek counsel, Absalom awaits to intercept with lies and innuendos: "You know, nobody up there cares about your concerns. But I do. Oh, if only I was in charge! I'd show everyone what justice is all about."

> Also, whenever anyone approached him to bow down before him, Absalom would reach out his hand, take hold of him and kiss him. Absalom behaved in this way toward all the Israelites who came to the

king asking for justice, and so he stole the hearts of the people of Israel. (15:5–6)

Absalom's smooching works perfectly. Little by little he undermines David's reputation and builds his own, until he's finally ready to make his big move. According to his plan, the trumpet sounds, announcing that he's now king. David is made aware of the widespread support for Absalom and the instability of his own situation. And as we've seen, David flees.

This good man is broken, fractured in his spirit. Not only has his son betrayed him, but David's feeling like there's no friend to be found. Picture the scene: He's scrambling around, throwing a few things in a bag, preparing to escape. After all these years, he'll once again be running for his life, just like those long years when he was a fugitive from Saul. *Been there, done that.*

If ever a man needed a sheltering tree, David now does.

The king's officials answered him, "Your servants are ready to do whatever our lord the king chooses."

The king set out, with his entire household following him; but he left ten concubines to take care of the palace. (15:15–16)

He "set out"—what emotion and pathos are woven into the fabric of those few words! David is leaving the great city of Zion—the place called the City of David. As he comes to the city's edge, he stops at the last house. With a breaking heart, he looks back over this place he's watched God build over the years. His mind is flooded with memories.

Friends and supporters and people of his household scurry past, leading beasts of burden piled high with belongings—they're all running for their lives.

David's in need of a tree to give him shelter—someone to say, "David, I'm here with you, here to stay. I don't have all the answers in this moment, but my heart goes out to you."

And God in His abundant grace sends this man a sheltering tree—in fact, God gives David five of them. Interestingly, most of us today hardly remember their names.

The first friend he encounters here is a foreigner (from Gath), and this is the first time he's mentioned in David's biography.

> All his men marched past him, along with all the Kerethites and Pelethites; and all the six hundred Gittites who had accompanied him from Gath marched before the king. The king said to Ittai the Gittite, "Why should you come along with us? Go back and stay with King Absalom. You are a foreigner, an exile from your homeland." (15:18–19)

Ittai the Gittite is a friend of the king. A Gittite was a person from Gath—which, as you'll remember, was Goliath's hometown. David has taken some of the Philistines into exile. Instead of hating him, however, they've fallen in love with him. Ittai is one of them.

Ittai is out of the limelight until the chips are down and David is stopped at that last house—when there's no more throne, no more glory. Suddenly, there's Ittai (with plenty others) coming alongside the king: "David, count me in. I'm with you all the way." How amazing that a person who was once an enemy is now a friend.

David tells him to take off. "This is your chance to stay safe. Go on back." He tells Ittai,

> "You came only yesterday. And today shall I make you wander about with us, when I do not know where I am going? Go back, and take your people with you. May the LORD show you kindness and faithfulness." (15:20)

He's saying, "It's gonna be hard where I'm going, so turn around, all of you. Shalom, brother."

> But Ittai replied to the king, "As surely as the LORD lives, and as my lord the king lives, wherever my lord the king may be, whether it means life or death, there will your servant be." (15:21)

That is a friend! "David, if they string you up, I'm putting my neck in the noose next to yours. If the whole world turns against you, I'll stand in your defense." Ittai was a man made of sturdy stuff. Not many friends are like that.

So David sends Ittai on ahead to join the march of David's loyal following. "Ittai the Gittite marched on with all his men and the families that were with him" (15:22).

As David and his fleeing followers push onward, the scene is a sad one:

The whole countryside wept aloud as all the people passed by. The king also crossed the Kidron Valley, and all the people moved on toward the wilderness. (15:23)

Then two more sheltering trees for David emerge—the priests Zadok and Abiathar, representatives of God who minister in the house of God.

Zadok was there, too, and all the Levites who were with him were carrying the ark of the covenant of God. They set down the ark of God, and Abiathar offered sacrifices until all the people had finished leaving the city. (15:24)

These two men come along carrying the ark of the covenant. They set down that heavy sacred chest, and look over at David. "We're with you, David. We've been with you all along. Now where do we go from here?"

Then the king said to Zadok, "Take the ark of God back into the city. If I find favor in the LORD's eyes, he will bring me back and let me see it and his dwelling place again. But if he says, 'I am not pleased with you,' then I am ready; let him do to me whatever seems good to him." (15:25–26)

What a teachable, humble spirit David has! That's how to ride out the whirlwind of consequences. "Lord, if You choose to finish me off, no problem. On the other hand, if You want to use me, I'm thrilled. Whatever happens, I abandon my future into Your hands."

Once again, David reveals through his obedience that he's a man after God's own heart. He knows that the ark of the covenant does not belong to him. Out of reverence and respect, he lays it all at the Lord's disposal, as this bit of commentary observes:

> David reveals a true understanding of the connection between the ark and God's presence with his people. He knows that possession of the ark does not guarantee God's blessing. . . . He also recognizes that the ark belongs in the capital city as a symbol of the Lord's rule over the nation . . . no matter who the king might be. David confesses that he has no exclusive claim to the throne and that Israel's divine King is free to confer the kingship on whomever he chooses.[23]

That's why David tells his buddies Zadok and Abiathar to take the ark back to Jerusalem. "Go back. You're needed there." In their loyalty, that's exactly what they did. No argument, no resistance; not even a discussion. They were there to help David, and if that meant going back, so be it.

Their presence in Jerusalem would mean their usefulness there as part of a messenger system to get David inside information about the conspirators and their plans:

> The king also said to Zadok the priest, ". . . Go back to the city with my blessing. Take your son Ahimaaz with you, and also Abiathar's son Jonathan. You and Abiathar return with your two sons. I will wait at the fords in the wilderness until word comes from you to inform me."
>
> So Zadok and Abiathar took the ark of God back to Jerusalem and stayed there. (15:27–29)

When you're really in need, true friends will say to you, "I'll do whatever you want me to. I'm available." They'll run interference for you. They stand in your corner.

The refugees keep going eastward from Jerusalem—and they and their leader are grieving:

> David continued up the Mount of Olives, weeping as he went; his head was covered and he was barefoot. All the people with him covered their heads too and were weeping as they went up. (15:30)

Picture that. The mighty king of Israel, barefoot, head covered, weeping aloud as he ascends this slope. The others are also dissolved in tears. It's a pathetic sight, but realistic.

Then another friend appears.

> When David arrived at the summit, where people used to worship God, Hushai the Arkite was there to meet him, his robe torn and dust on his head. (15:32)

Who is Hushai? Later in this passage he's called "David's friend" (15:37 NASB)—that says it all. He's another sheltering tree for David.

Hushai's clothing is torn and his head covered with dust. That's what people did in those days to show their total bankruptcy or grief—as if to say, "I have nothing left. I'm finished." For Hushai, these were marks of his compassionate feeling for David. And David spots it immediately. And he gives this loyal friend a very significant task. David is getting his secret messenger network set up to furnish him with inside information on Absalom's plans—plus he has a plan for negating the influence of Absalom's wisest counselor, a man named Ahithophel.

David tells this to Hushai:

> "If you go with me, you will be a burden to me. But if you return to the city and say to Absalom, 'Your Majesty, I will be your servant; I was your father's servant in the past, but now I will be your servant,' then you can help me by frustrating Ahithophel's advice. Won't the priests Zadok and Abiathar be there with you? Tell them anything you hear in the king's palace. Their two sons . . . are there with them. Send them to me with anything you hear."
>
> So Hushai, David's confidant, arrived at Jerusalem as Absalom was entering the city. (15:33–37)

Hushai will now be David's spy in Absalom's camp. Here we're seeing David as the consummate military strategist. In the midst of all his misery, he's still able to strategize wisely.

That whole line of communication that gets set up—thanks to the willing services of David's loyal friends—will soon lead to David's survival and Absalom's overthrow. When the chips are down, these loyal hearts rally around their king, David. God bless those unknowns!

We meet another group of sheltering trees for David and the exiles fleeing with him as they near an out-of-the-way place called Mahanaim:

> Shobi son of Nahash . . . and Makir son of Ammiel . . . and Barzillai the Gileadite . . . brought bedding and bowls and articles of pottery. They also brought wheat and barley, flour and roasted grain, beans and lentils, honey and curds, sheep, and cheese from cows' milk for David and his people to eat. For they said, "The people have become exhausted and hungry and thirsty in the wilderness." (17:27–29)

Shobi, Maki, and Barzillai—more nobodies who became a group of somebodies in David's corner.

Mahanaim, where David and those with him arrive, is in the wilderness. It's the place where, centuries earlier, angels of God met the sojourning Jacob, and he called the place "God's camp" (Genesis 32:1–2). Here's David out in the middle of nowhere, and now the angels come in the form of these three men—Shobi, Makir, Barzillai—who bring them abundant food and supplies. It is God's camp again.

We learn later that Barzillai, by the way, is eighty years old (2 Samuel 19:32). He could have said, "I'm old, I've served my time, I'm retired. Let somebody younger help David." But he didn't say that.

When you're hungry and weary and thirsty in the wilderness, that's when true friends come through! You don't even have to ask. When you have friends like this, they know when you're hungry, thirsty, weary. Sheltering friends don't have to be told what to do, the practical stuff. They just do it. This is faith in action, rubber-meets-the-road Christianity.

Sometime later, another friend—Joab—shows his loyalty to David in a unique way. We've seen how grief-stricken David was after receiving word about Absalom's death. This happens before David has a chance to be reconciled with his son and come to terms about their differences—and also before David can express his sorrow for being negligent as a father. The news of Absalom's death is a crushing blow, and David's world caves in. We see and hear the anguish of his sorrow as he cries out again, "O Absalom, Absalom, my son, my son!"

David couldn't get past this grief. He was caught in an emotional vortex that paralyzed him. Sometimes grief does that to a person.

Joab was told, "The king is weeping and mourning for Absalom." And for the whole army the victory that day was turned into mourning, because on that day the troops heard it said, "The king is grieving for his son." (19:1–2)

David's loyal soldiers, who had fought so hard to defeat Absalom's rebels, are seeing Absalom's death as God's deliverance. Now David can get back on the throne where he belongs—God has vindicated His true chosen king.

But David is so consumed in his personal grief that he loses awareness of his army's condition and morale, and their needs.

At this point, Joab confronts his king—and does so with the bold force needed in the moment:

Then Joab went into the house to the king and said, "Today you have humiliated all your men, who have just saved your life and the lives of your sons and daughters and the lives of your wives and concubines. You love those who hate you and hate those who love you. You have made it clear today that the commanders and their men mean nothing to you. I see that you would be pleased if Absalom were alive today and all of us were dead. Now go out and encourage your men. I swear by the LORD that if you don't go out, not a man will be left with you by nightfall. This will be worse for you than all the calamities that have come on you from your youth till now." (19:5–7)

Here we have a friend's strong rebuke combined with a friend's wise counsel. Joab is speaking the truth in love. "David, get on your feet! You've got to get past this grief. Your men have risked their lives in their loyalty to you. They've believed in you and defended you. You've licked your wounds long enough! Your heart may be broken, but you're still the king of Israel, and there's a job to be done!"

Joab cared enough to confront him, and to prevent him from compounding the damage already done.

We have to hand it to David here. Though gripped by grief, he listens to Joab. He takes his friend's advice and gets back to work leading his army and his people as their king.

> So the king got up and took his seat in the gateway. When the men were
> told, "The king is sitting in the gateway," they all came before him. (19:8)

The gateway was where the king would meet with the people to give them guidance, justice, counsel, and so on. With David back in the gateway, people knew he was back in leadership.

Joab's sheltering friendship, like all the others who'd ministered to him earlier, has helped lift David up when he bottomed out.

TRUTH ABOUT FRIENDSHIP

Friendship is where we find the hands of God ministering, encouraging, giving, and supporting, even through relatively unknown heroes of the faith—nobodies like Ittai the Gittite, Zadok, Abiathar, Hushai, Shobi, Makir, and Barzillai, as well as prominent, loyal leaders like Joab.

You may be surprised to know, as I was, that the words *friends, friendly,* and *friendship* appear over a hundred times in the Scriptures. God says a lot about friends. As I read through the verses and think about true friendship, I believe it all boils down to these four things.

1. *Friends are not optional; they're essential.* There's no substitute for a friend—someone to care, to listen, to feel, to comfort—and, yes, occasionally, to reprove. True friends do that best.

2. *Friends are not automatic; they must be cultivated.* The Bible says, "A man who has friends must himself be friendly" (Proverbs 18:24 NKJV). As Samuel Johnson wrote: "One should keep his friendship in a constant repair."[24] As with trees, friendship needs cultivation.

3. *Friends are not neutral in their influence; they impact our lives.* If your friends lead good lives, they encourage you to become a better person. If

your friends lead disreputable lives, they lead you down their harmful path. "Do not be deceived: 'Bad company corrupts good morals'" (1 Corinthians 15:33 NASB). So choose your friends carefully and wisely. Gossips usually gravitate to gossips. Rebels run with rebels. You want to be wise? Choose wise friends.

4. *Friendships come in varying degrees, some of whom play more significant roles in our life than others.* Most of us have many acquaintances, some casual friends, a few close friends, and even fewer intimate friends. Let's think about some of those categories.

With close friends, we share similar life goals, plus the ability to discuss life's hard questions. We do projects together, exercise together, socialize together, and sometimes even vacation together.

With more intimate friends, we tend to have more regular contact and deeper commitment. We're open and vulnerable with these people, and we're eager for their counsel. Intimate friends are just as free to criticize and to correct as they are to embrace and encourage, because trust and mutual understanding has been established between them.

All levels of friendship are important, but the most important, of course, are intimate friends. We all need at least one person with whom we can be open and honest; we all need at least one person who offers us the shelter of support and encouragement as well as hard truths and confrontation. Sheltering trees, all!

Thankfully, David had a grove of such trees. As a result he made it through the toughest days and loneliest hours of his life.

If you have such friends, this is a good time to call or meet with them and enjoy their shelter. If you don't have such friends—this is a good time to plant the seeds for some. You'll never regret it.

Just ask David.

GOING AFTER GOD'S OWN HEART: From David's Psalm 16, make his prayer your own:

> Preserve me, O God, for in you I take refuge.
> I say to the LORD, "You are my Lord;
> I have no good apart from you."
> As for the saints in the land, they are the excellent ones,
> in whom is all my delight. (16:1–3 ESV)

CHAPTER 21

BIG ENOUGH TO FORGIVE

One of the many qualities that made David a man after God's own heart is his forgiving spirit.

It happens to be one of our most difficult attributes to acquire. Instead of fully forgiving someone, most of us opt for one of three different responses.

1. We offer *conditional* forgiveness. "I will forgive you *if . . .*" Or, "I'll forgive you *as soon as . . .*" If the offender will come back to us and make things right, and own up to their part of the problem—then we'll forgive them. That's conditional forgiveness. We're waiting like a tiger swishing his tail. "You make your move, then I'll determine whether it's time to back away or pounce and bite."

2. We sometimes offer *partial* forgiveness. "I forgive you, but don't expect me to forget." Or, "I forgive you—but get out of my life." Or, "I'll forgive you—until it happens again."

3. Or we practice *delayed* forgiveness. "I'll forgive you, someday—just give me time." This is a common reaction of someone who has been hurt deeply, and who has nursed that hurt over the years.

Most of us would rather sit on a judgment seat than a mercy seat. If somebody wronged us, we'd rather watch him squirm in misery than smile in relief.

Yet forgiveness isn't just about the other person; it's also about *us*. When we're unforgiving, it has a dramatic, downward effect on our own life.

First of all, if there isn't forgiveness after the offense, resentment begins to build. Resentment unchecked leads to hatred and holding a grudge. And sustained hatred can then lead to seeking revenge. We bide our time: "When my chance comes, I'll get even."

I openly confess that years ago I couldn't have written this chapter. I hadn't really come to terms with these things in my own life. Thank God, He has helped me deal with this, and today I can honestly say I don't know of an individual I haven't forgiven. I write that with no sense of pride; who am I to brag, having nursed an unforgiving spirit far too long? I say that with thankfulness and relief, and in humble honesty to encourage you to know that it can happen.

Now let me go a step further. I still wrestle with this issue on a regular basis. Every week, it seems, I have to come to terms with not letting some offense linger and lead me back into resentment. I have to deal with it quickly, or I'm a goner. Otherwise, I'd soon be all the way to revenge.

DAVID FORGIVES

When his son Absalom usurped his throne, David reached his life's lowest ebb. It may very well have been at this moment in his life that he wrote these words:

> I waited patiently for the LORD;
> he turned to me and heard my cry.
> He lifted me out of the slimy pit,
> out of the mud and mire;
> he set my feet on a rock
> and gave me a firm place to stand. . . .
> For troubles without number surround me;
> my sins have overtaken me, and I cannot see.
> They are more than the hairs of my head,
> and my heart fails within me. (Psalm 40:1–2,12)

In this desperate moment—this pit of mud and mire and of "troubles without number," and with guilt for his sins overwhelming David—a man named Shimei comes out of nowhere to add to his misery. Shimei is distantly related to Saul. To David, he is no friend, no "sheltering tree." To put it bluntly, he's a jerk, a real loser who's more than willing to hit a person when he's down. Alexander Whyte called him "a reptile of the royal house of Saul."[25]

It's when David is fleeing eastward from Jerusalem (where Absalom has taken control) that he encounters this reptile:

> As King David approached Bahurim, a man from the same clan as Saul's family came out from there. His name was Shimei son of Gera, and he cursed as he came out. He pelted David and all the king's officials with stones, though all the troops and the special guard were on David's right and left. As he cursed, Shimei said, "Get out, get out, you murderer, you scoundrel! The LORD has repaid you for all the blood you shed in the household of Saul, in whose place you have reigned. The LORD has given the kingdom into the hands of your son Absalom. You have come to ruin because you are a murderer!" (2 Samuel 16:5–8)

In the New Living Translation, this last part reads:

> "The LORD is paying you back for all the bloodshed in Saul's clan. You stole his throne [which we know is a lie], and now the LORD has given it to your son Absalom. At last you will taste some of your own medicine, for you are a murderer!" (16:8)

Shimei was your basic reprobate—the kind of guy who hits you below the belt, and when you squirm, he comes back with another blow.

Then along comes a loyal supporter to give David counsel: "Abishai son of Zeruiah said to the king, 'Why should this dead dog curse my lord the king? Let me go over and cut off his head'" (16:9).

That's a pretty direct game plan, I'd say. Maybe you've received that kind of advice from a friend who sees you being treated unfairly: "Let me handle him! I'm good at this." Or, "Just sue the guy! After all, you've got your rights. Stand up for yourself, don't let him walk all over you!" (Sound familiar?)

Shimei has thrown rocks at David, he's cursed him, and he's lied about him in this personal attack. He's way out of line. David has done nothing to warrant these public assaults. Nevertheless, they've come. David now has a choice. He can be offended and become resentful and pursue revenge—or not.

The king tells Abishai, "What does this have to do with you . . . ? If he is cursing because the LORD said to him, 'Curse David,' who can ask, 'Why do you do this?'" (16:10).

David is refusing to retaliate. He stays calm and doesn't allow Shimei's short fuse to cause an explosion.

The king turns, and with a wave of his hand, he addresses all those who are fleeing with him:

"My son, my own flesh and blood, is trying to kill me. How much more, then, this Benjamite! Leave him alone; let him curse, for the LORD has told him to. It may be that the LORD will look upon my misery and restore to me his covenant blessing instead of his curse today." (16:11–12)

It's an amazing study in self-control. Shimei attacks him in multiple ways, but instead of fighting back, David says, "The Lord is in it." He doesn't get offended. He doesn't take it personally. He doesn't even yell! How does he do that?

Soft heart and thick skin—that's the ticket, plain and simple.

Let me tell you, if you hope to be used of God, you need skin that's rhinoceros thick, so that you can get punched around without losing control. You get the job done while overlooking all those hurtful little comments people are going to make. Count on it, people like Shimei are out there by the dozens! Such "reptiles" proliferate. And when you walk through their thorns, you have to wear heavy boots. Especially if you're called into leadership, always dealing with people, you have to be well-shod and armorplated. If not, you're doomed to failure.

Now that doesn't mean a thickness toward God. But it does mean you have to decide: When I encounter someone like this Shimei, am I going to be offended or not? Am I big enough to forgive? Or will I reduce myself to his size and sling rocks back?

SEEING BOTH SIDES

Let's jump ahead in the story. After Absalom's forces are defeated, and Absalom lives no longer, David and those who fled with him are on their westward journey back to Jerusalem. As they prepare to cross the Jordan River, they are met by "men of Judah" (19:15) who wish to assist the king in his return to reclaim the throne.

And wouldn't you know it? Once again, here comes Shimei.

When Shimei son of Gera crossed the Jordan, he fell prostrate before the king and said to him, "May my lord not hold me guilty. Do not remember how your servant did wrong on the day my lord the king left Jerusalem. May the king put it out of his mind. For I your servant know that I have sinned, but today I have come here as the first from the tribes of Joseph to come down and meet my lord the king." (19:18–20)

Shimei acknowledges that he "did wrong"—"I have sinned." His words of apology must have rung a bell in David's mind. Not many years earlier, he'd said those same words to Nathan.

Forgiveness comes easier when we remember times in our own past when we failed and were forgiven.

Before we look closer at David's response, consider the other side of the equation. Think about being in Shimei's shoes. He's not some Old Testament caricature; his actions and reactions are real. We know that, because we've all had similar experiences, haven't we? We've done or said something that could easily offend another person. What we did was wrong, and we know the other person is hung up on that. So the ball's in our court. It's our move now, and we need to come to terms with it. But that's tough, isn't it? And it's even tougher when we know we were 100 percent in the wrong.

That's where Shimei finds himself in this scene.

Let's turn again to David's side of the matter. After Shimei's confession, David could easily treat him with indifference. He could just ignore the man—look past him with a shrug. But indifference is certainly not forgiveness; indifference is rage controlled.

As Shimei is spread out on the ground before David, and saying, "I have sinned"—what he's really saying is, "Will you please forgive me?"

Once again, Abishai is there beside David, ready with heated counsel regarding this jerk Shimei: "Shouldn't Shimei be put to death for this? He cursed the LORD's anointed" (19:21).

He's saying, "Don't forget, David—this guy kicked you when you were down. Now give him the same treatment. Kick this loser hard and finish him off."

This time again, David isn't swayed by vengeful counsel. He tells Abishai,

"What does this have to do with you . . . ? What right do you have to interfere? Should anyone be put to death in Israel today? Don't I know that today I am king over Israel?"

So the king said to Shimei, "You shall not die." And the king promised him on oath. (19:22–23)

"You shall not die"—David had heard these same words, spoken by God's prophet Nathan, after confessing his sins in the matter of Bathsheba and Uriah.

How can David forgive a reptile like this Shimei? First of all, he keeps his vertical focus clear. He knows God can handle Shimei's transgression; God is good at taking care of offenses.

When I'm on the receiving end of some offense, I've discovered great strength in taking it immediately to God. And I mean *immediately*. There's something very stabilizing in getting vertical perspective on a situation before seeking any horizontal counsel.

Second, David is very much aware of his own failures. The humbled forgiven make good forgivers. David knows only too well what it means to be a sinner. He knows what it means to be forgiven by the Lord. He knows the heartache of having done wrong, and the cleansing feeling—the relief, the sense of burden lifted—that follows repentance and forgiveness. Those horrible months when he was humbled before his God have seasoned David and made him merciful. Being well aware of his own shortcomings gives him great patience with another's wrongdoing.

The proud have a hard time forgiving. Those who've never recognized their own failures have a tough time tolerating, understanding, and forgiving the failure of others.

SOUND ADVICE ON FORGIVENESS

If we're to develop a spirit of forgiveness in our own lives and put forgiveness into action, we need to do several things.

1. *We must cultivate a thicker skin, a buffer to take those jolts that come our way.* We need to ask for God's help with this. "Lord, help me not to be so sensitive, so thin-skinned. Lord, take away this delicate china-doll mentality of mine, and give me depth. Toughen my hide. Calm my responses. Make me patient with those who speak too quickly. Make me like Christ." This will help us keep our sense of balance so that the slightest push doesn't topple us over. We can bounce back from whatever hits us.

2. *We can try to understand where the offender is coming from.* This takes a lot of grace—but again, God is good at grace. Try to see beyond the offense and find the little boy inside that man lashing out at you, or the little girl inside that woman who's striking back. Try to find out what's behind their offensive words or behavior. You may be surprised how helpful this can be. Who knows? David may have seen a touch of his old immature self in Shimei, as those rocks came whizzing by.

Our Savior did this even while hanging on the cross. He looked at His accusers and executioners and prayed, "Father, forgive them, for they do not know what they are doing" (Luke 23:34). In that one statement, we realize how our Lord viewed His enemies.

3. *We should recall times in our own life when we've needed forgiveness, and then apply the same emotion.* All of us, at one time or another, have done or said something dumb or extreme or offensive, and have needed someone's forgiveness. This happens between friends, within families, at work, at school, and yes, even at church. We must be candid about this—nobody is above the drag of humanity. When offenses hit us, we can be as ugly or vile or ornery as the other guy, and we need to confess it openly.

I pray for this kind of authenticity all the time. "Keep me authentic, Lord. Take every phony-baloney cell out of my body. Just keep me real."

4. *We need to verbalize our forgiveness.* Say it, don't just think it. Spoken words of forgiveness and graciousness are marvelously therapeutic to the offender, no matter how small or great the offense. Saying our feelings removes all doubt.

Our typical human response to offense is to try all the wrong things: silence, resentment, grudge, indifference, even plotting a way to maneuver and manipulate to get our offender in a vulnerable spot so we can twist the verbal knife, once we've plunged it in. None of this pleases God. Nor does it work.

Cultivating a forgiving spirit is a challenge for every one of us. We need a heart full of forgiveness and grace in our family relationships, in our work and school relationships, and certainly in our church relationships. We need to put feet to the hope that's within us. We need to respond to the flaws of others with Christlike grace and complete forgiveness.

Like David, we need a soft heart and thick skin, and a vertical focus, and full awareness of our own failures and need for forgiveness.

GOING AFTER GOD'S OWN HEART: From David's Psalm 25, make his prayer your own:

> Remember, LORD, your great mercy and love,
> for they are from of old.
> Do not remember the sins of my youth
> and my rebellious ways;
> according to your love remember me,
> for you, LORD, are good. (25:6–7)

CHAPTER 22

SONG OF TRIUMPH

The long shadows of age and pressure are beginning to fall across David's face as he enters his twilight years. He has lived a full life and experienced both the heights and the depths. He has often had to trust God in impossible circumstances.

Long before he was a king, David was a singer of songs, and in 2 Samuel 22 we find what I'm convinced is his last song. Three major events in David's life have provided preparation for this song.

As we've seen, David suffered the anguish and grief of the premature death of his son Absalom, who was murdered after leading a conspiracy against his father. The second blow driving David to his knees was a three-year famine that struck the land. And finally, Israel has gone back to war with their age-old enemy the Philistines: "Once again there was a battle between the Philistines and Israel. David went down with his men to fight against the Philistines, and he became exhausted" (2 Samuel 21:15).

After all he's been through, who wouldn't feel exhausted? David's only human. The loss of a son, the suffering brought on by famine, the misery of battle—all this wears on him until David begins to crack.

The weary David thus lifts his hands to God and declares his feelings in the song we find in 2 Samuel 22. But the tone isn't what you might expect, given his circumstances. It's not a dark and somber dirge from this gifted composer, but a psalm of praise to the One so deserving of it: "David sang to the LORD the words of this song" (22:1).

It's a song that mentions hardships David has known: "violent people"

(22:3), "waves of death" and "torrents of destruction" (22:5), a "powerful enemy" and "the day of my disaster" (22:18–19). But throughout these struggles, David has known God's deliverance: "He rescued me. . . . The LORD was my support" (22:18–19).

David in this psalm of praise sums up his full life in four themes, four expressions that weave their way through the words.

GOD'S SECURITY IN OUR TOUGH TIMES

The first theme: When times are tough, God is our only security.

David sings:

> The LORD is my rock, my fortress and my deliverer;
> my God is my rock, in whom I take refuge,
> my shield and the horn of my salvation.
> He is my stronghold, my refuge and my savior. (2 Samuel
>   22:2–3)

Each of these poetic expressions carries a unique and powerful meaning in which David describes the Lord as a secure heavenly Father. "Times are tough," this weary man is saying; "I've lost my son, I'm losing my nation, my army's in disarray. My land and my people must once again face warfare as the Philistines come upon us. And yet I find that the Lord continues to be my shield, my stronghold, my refuge."

Feel what David is describing:

> In my distress I called to the LORD;
> I called out to my God.
> From his temple he heard my voice;
> my cry came to his ears. (22:7)

God is no distant deity to David, preoccupied elsewhere. His God heard his voice! Those guttural cries came into His ears! And watch God's response:

The earth trembled and quaked,
the foundations of the heavens shook;
they trembled because he was angry.
Smoke rose from his nostrils;
consuming fire came from his mouth,
burning coals blazed out of it.
He parted the heavens and came down;
dark clouds were under his feet.
He mounted the cherubim and flew;
he soared on the wings of the wind.
He made darkness his canopy around him—
the dark rain clouds of the sky. (22:8–12)

What is God doing? He's responding to David's cries by bringing him help.

Out of the brightness of his presence
bolts of lightning blazed forth.
The LORD thundered from heaven;
the voice of the Most High resounded.
He shot his arrows and scattered the enemy,
with great bolts of lightning he routed them.
The valleys of the sea were exposed
and the foundations of the earth laid bare
at the rebuke of the LORD,
at the blast of breath from his nostrils.
He reached down from on high and took hold of me;
he drew me out of deep waters.
He rescued me from my powerful enemy,
from my foes, who were too strong for me.
They confronted me in the day of my disaster. (22:13–19)

When David is beaten and broken, the hateful enemy invades and confronts and deals harshly, without mercy. But tenderly and surely the Lord brings reprieve and relief:

The LORD was my support.
He brought me out into a spacious place;
he rescued me because he delighted in me. (22:19–20)

Isn't that magnificent? We have no trouble believing the words about calamity and strong enemies and distress and death and destruction and violence—but it's so difficult in those times to believe that the Lord actually *delights* in us. Yet He does. That's the whole message of grace. The Lord dispatches His angels of hope who bring invincible help because He finds delight in us. He cares for us. He feels our ache. He feels it deeply. Even though we resist it, it's true: He delights in us. Believe it, my friend!

Are days of trouble upon you? When times are tough, the Lord is our only security. David assures us in his song of the Lord's delight in us and His care for us in what's happening in our lives, this very moment. What encouragement that brings as the battle exhausts us!

GOD'S LIGHT IN OUR DARKNESS

The second theme in David's song: When our days are dark, the Lord is our only light.

You, LORD, are my lamp;
the LORD turns my darkness into light. (2 Samuel 22:29)

In our darkness, the Lord gives us enough light so we can see to take the next step. That's all He gives—and, in reality, that's all we need.

Step by step, again and again, David has seen the Lord illumine his darkness. Look at what else David experiences:

With your help I can advance against a troop;
with my God I can scale a wall. (22:30)

"I can see my way, Lord—I can get over these hurdles because You're the lamp that shows me the way."

Remember the encouraging words from David that we hear in another song of illumination, Psalm 27: "The LORD is my light and my salvation." We can read that last word also as *deliverer* or *deliverance*, in our times of hardship and need and danger:

> The LORD is my light and my salvation [my deliverance]—
> whom shall I fear?
> The LORD is the stronghold of my life—
> of whom shall I be afraid? (Psalm 27:1)

The Lord is our deliverance and our defense. David goes on in Psalm 27 to describe different experiences and circumstances in which the Lord gives deliverance. He even says, "Though my father and mother forsake me, the LORD will receive me" (27:10). It's true—the Lord enlightens our way even more than our parents ever could. The light of the Lord provides both direction and deliverance, so why should we fear?

All of us have our own particular fears—of darkness, the unknown, failure, inadequacy, financial disaster, sickness, death. You name it, we experience it. Yet the Lord, faithful and trustworthy, promises to deliver us from all our fears. So it stands to reason we can rest in Him:

> As for God, his way is perfect:
> The LORD's word is flawless;
> he shields all who take refuge in him. (2 Samuel 22:31)

He shields us when we go to Him for protection. What a wonderful message of hope!

GOD'S STRENGTH IN OUR WEAKNESS

Here's the third theme we find in 2 Samuel 22: When our walk is weak, the Lord is our only strength.

> For who is God besides the LORD?

And who is the Rock except our God?
It is God who arms me with strength
and keeps my way secure. (22:32–33)

Clearly, David is not thinking of his own inherent strength—remember, he was exhausted from the battle. Rather, he's saying here, "*The Lord* is my strength." And it is varied strength, in many dimensions:

He makes my feet like the feet of a deer;
he causes me to stand on the heights.
He trains my hands for battle;
my arms can bend a bow of bronze. (22:34–35)

With that kind of strength—sourced in God—we can face whatever life throws at us.

David goes on to vividly describe specific instances of weakness in which the Lord gives strength. When times are tough, the Lord sees us through. When days are dark, the Lord is the light. When our walk is weak, the Lord is our strength. The apostle Paul echoed the same thing:

I was given a thorn in my flesh, a messenger of Satan, to torment me. Three times I pleaded with the Lord to take it away from me. But he said to me, "My grace is sufficient for you, for my power is made perfect in weakness." Therefore I will boast all the more gladly about my weaknesses, so that Christ's power may rest on me. That is why, for Christ's sake, I delight in weaknesses, in insults, in hardships, in persecutions, in difficulties. For when I am weak, then I am strong. (2 Corinthians 12:7–10)

That's the secret: God's great power is perfected in our utter weakness. He tells us, "*My* power is best displayed when *you* are weak." But that's hard to put into action, isn't it? We want to be strong in ourselves. And yet a key principle in the Christian life is that God is never stronger in His work than when we are admittedly weak. When we come to an end in ourselves, He steps up and shows Himself strong. David sings it out in these words:

You make your saving help my shield;
your help has made me great. (22:36)

God's personal help is the only source of David's greatness, David's success. That's the truth for us all. When times are tough, the Lord is our only security. When our walk is weak, the Lord is our only strength.

OUR ONLY HOPE IN UNCERTAINTY

The fourth theme here is this: When our future looks foggy or fuzzy, the Lord is our only hope. Look at the grand finale to David's song:

Therefore I will praise you, LORD, among the nations;
I will sing the praises of your name. (2 Samuel 22:50)

Despite all that David has been through, he isn't bitter or resentful. He approaches the end of his life with a song on his lips, not grumblings or regrets, because he knows this truth about the Lord:

He gives his king great victories;
he shows unfailing kindness to his anointed,
to David and his descendants forever. (22:51)

I've noticed that as we get older and the years start to stack up, the future becomes far more significant than the present. In midlife we begin to wonder about what our old age will be like, should we live that long. In this song, David promises us—from both experience and faith—that the Lord will show loving-kindness to His anointed and even take care of their descendants forever. That's a hope-filled vision—and the Lord is the only source for that true hope.

We Christians frequently have trouble believing that God is our only hope, security, light, and strength, because we're so prone to try everything else. We automatically depend upon everything *except* the Lord. Yet still He waits there for us—patiently waiting to show Himself strong.

He *is* our light and our salvation; whom should we fear? God hears our cry and lifts us out of a horrible pit; He places our feet upon a rock and establishes our pathway. He proves Himself strong in our weakness, He sheds light in our darkness, He becomes hope in our uncertainty and security in our confusion. He's the centerpiece of our lives.

Thank you, David, for leaving us this reminder in your final song of triumph. More than that, thank You, Lord, for being there throughout our lives, never letting us down, never making us feel foolish because we're weak.

Whom have we, Lord, but You?

———

GOING AFTER GOD'S OWN HEART: From David's Psalm 28, make his prayer your own:

> Praise be to the LORD,
> for he has heard my cry for mercy.
> The LORD is my strength and my shield;
> my heart trusts in him, and he helps me.
> My heart leaps for joy,
> and with my song I praise him. (28:6–7)

CHAPTER 23

WHEN THE GODLY ARE FOOLISH

Wouldn't it be wonderful if we were guaranteed to automatically grow wiser as we grow older? Or to automatically be more immune to sin the longer we walk with the Lord?

That's not the case, however. Age alone is no guarantee of maturity or freedom from error. As Elihu said to Job, "The experts have no corner on wisdom; getting old doesn't guarantee good sense" (Job 32:9 MSG). And we'll never be immune to sin's appeal. Often those who fall hardest are those who've walked with God longest. There's no such thing as outgrowing sin. Not until we're with the Lord in eternity will we be what we ought to be—pure and righteous and sinless.

In 2 Samuel 24 (and its parallel passage, 1 Chronicles 21), we're given a vivid account of a tragic example of late-life error. David, advanced in years, committed a sin that tragically affected thousands of lives.

BEHIND A BAD DECISION

This event probably takes place on the heels of the reignited conflict we've noted between Israel and the Philistines. Understandably, King David is anxious to ensure Israel's continued military strength. Perhaps also he lets down his spiritual guard after Israel's latest victories. As we've noted, we're most vulnerable immediately after victory; that's when Satan springs his traps. And David is vulnerable.

Let's explore what happens:

> The anger of the LORD burned against Israel, and he incited David against them, saying, "Go and take a census of Israel and Judah." (2 Samuel 24:1)

God is angry with Israel. We don't know exactly why, but whatever the reason, it has David ticked off too. Upset and hassled, he commands his army leaders to take a military census:

> So the king said to Joab and the army commanders with him, "Go throughout the tribes of Israel from Dan to Beersheba and enroll the fighting men, so that I may know how many there are." (24:2)

Bible scholars suggest that while David's stated goal is simply to count his fighting men, his unstated motive is pride. He apparently wants to see (and report) the impressive size and strength of the military forces under his command.

At this point he receives some wise pushback—which, unfortunately, he ignored:

> But Joab replied to the king, "May the LORD your God multiply the troops a hundred times over, and may the eyes of my lord the king see it. But why does my lord the king want to do such a thing?" (24:3)

This was a gracious way of saying, "David, why do you insist on doing this?" By raising the question, Joab is suggesting a reconsideration of this move. But David never gets it. Or if he does, his response isn't revealed; he seems to pull rank and say to Joab, "Do as I say."

In 1 Chronicles, we're given more insight into the decision: "Satan rose up against Israel and incited David to take a census of Israel" (1 Chronicles 21:1).

That's a mind-boggling statement! Satan, our spiritual enemy, was directly responsible for impressing David's mind with this wayward thought. However, this need not be surprising, since we know that the real spiritual battle for our lives occurs in the mind. As the apostle Paul said about Satan's work, "We are not ignorant of his schemes" (2 Corinthians 2:11 NASB). The Greek term rendered there as "schemes" has in its root the word *mind*. The verse could be paraphrased, "We are not ignorant of Satan's ability to get into our minds and direct our thoughts."

That's exactly what's happens to David. Satan nudges him in his private thoughts and says, "Why don't you number these people? Let's see how big your kingdom is, and your army. Why not take an inventory that you can be proud of?"

David's first weakness here is being out of touch with God. We don't find him praying, seeking God's counsel, or searching the Scriptures before he makes this decision. He simply decides to do it. David's second weakness is being unaccountable to anyone around him—a dangerous oversight.

Although Joab warns him, "the king's word prevailed against Joab" (1 Chronicles 21:4 NASB). This suggests there might have been something of an argument between these two, king versus general—and the king won out. Nevertheless, Joab is far more in line with God's perspective on what David is ordering done: "This command was . . . evil in the sight of God" (21:7).

David has reached such a peerless position as king of Israel that he answers to nobody. He can do whatever he wants, virtually without challenge. Even when it comes to someone as influential and important as the commander of his entire army, David can say, "Just do it!" Right or wrong, his word stands. An unaccountable life is a dangerous life, regardless of the high-ranking position anyone holds. It's a precarious place to be. But that's where David is.

If you find yourself in that trusted and precarious position of being unquestioned in your authority, be very, very careful. In fact, I would counsel you to select a small group of trusted people to whom you voluntarily make yourself accountable. Carte blanche, free-wheeling leadership is dangerous. Few people can handle it. In this case, not even an experienced godly king named David could handle it. His decision to number the people reveals this.

Sustained leadership that stays on track in pleasing God is never easy. In his book *Spiritual Leadership*, J. Oswald Sanders opened the chapter called "The Cost of Leadership" with this statement:

To aspire to leadership in God's kingdom requires us to be willing to pay a price higher than others are willing to pay. The toll of true leadership is heavy, and the more effective the leadership, the greater the cost.[26]

When a spiritual leader doesn't pay the price—when he wanders from the things of God—the consequences are often devastating and always far-reaching. When men and women who claim to model the message of Christ defect from that message, either by their actions or the statements that fall from their lips, they leave a destructive wake in the body of Christ.

BEHIND A TROUBLED HEART

The king's sinful decision gets carried out by Joab and the army commanders. It's a lengthy task:

> After they had gone through the entire land, they came back to Jerusalem at the end of nine months and twenty days.
>
> Joab reported the number of the fighting men to the king. (2 Samuel 24:8–9)

Look at what follows: "David was conscience-stricken after he had counted the fighting men" (24:10).

That's why David was a man after God's heart. He wasn't perfect, but to the end of his days he has a sensitive heart for God. "David's heart *troubled* him" (24:10 NASB)—the Hebrew term is *nakah*, and it's a severe word, meaning "to be attacked, to be assaulted." On occasion it's used in reference to a city that's destroyed or slaughtered. It conveys the idea of being wounded or crippled. Deep inside David's inner man there's a disturbing sense of God's displeasure over what he has done.

When we experience that inner troubling, we're on our way to recovery. But many are the stubborn saints who knowingly step out against God's will, only to run faster and faster, refusing to listen to the troubled heart inside. Regrettably, those with the greatest power and influence are often listening the least to that inner, aching voice.

David shows that he still has spiritual sensitivity. When he gets the census numbers from Joab and begins to study the report, perhaps the Lord brings back to mind Joab's original resistance to this thing. A question begins to haunt David: *Why have I done this thing?* The longer he thinks about it, the louder the answer pulsates through his brain: *My own pride is the only reason.*

Have you ever been troubled by something in your spiritual walk? If so, what have you done about it? Have you ignored it and just kept going in the same direction? Or did you come to a dead stop and say, "I was wrong. *Wrong!* God is dealing with me about this, and I know what He wants me to do about it."

David's heart is troubled after numbering the people, and once again we find the man saying those hard words:

> David . . . said to the LORD, "I have sinned greatly in what I have done. Now, LORD, I beg you, take away the guilt of your servant. I have done a very foolish thing." (24:10)

When we've done wrong and we begin to see the devastation that results from our sin, we cannot let it rest—at least not long, if we're sensitive to God's dealing with us.

That's pretty honest, isn't it? "I have sinned greatly . . . I have done a very foolish thing."

After this genuine declaration, David has a choice to make. This is a most unusual section of Scripture. It's the only time I know of in the Bible where a person is given the opportunity to choose the consequences of following wrong.

God gives David three choices.

> The LORD said to Gad, David's seer, "Go and tell David, 'This is what the LORD says: I am giving you three options. Choose one of them for me to carry out against you.'"
>
> So Gad went to David and said to him, "This is what the LORD says: 'Take your choice: three years of famine, three months of being swept away before your enemies, with their swords overtaking you, or three days

of the sword of the LORD—days of plague in the land, with the angel of the LORD ravaging every part of Israel.' Now then, decide how I should answer the one who sent me." (1 Chronicles 21:9–12)

Now that's tough, isn't it? Any one of the three choices is awful. But what a clear reminder for us: One does not sin without making waves and causing a wake. Even if David chooses the three-day plague (as he does), it's a never-to-be-forgotten event.

What a deterrent to sin it would be if, before the fact, we could be given a glimpse of its impact—the sorrow and grief it will bring to others, the toll it will take.

I'm not surprised at all to read how David first responded to Gad: "I am in deep distress" (2 Samuel 24:14).

The Hebrew word here for "distress" is *tsarar*; it means "to be tied up, restricted, cramped." David's stomach is cramped up and churning inside. We would say he's tied up in knots. (We've all felt that way.) David hears this judgment, and the tremendous guilt he feels down inside is almost more than he can bear.

He makes his decision and shares it with Gad: "Let me fall into the hands of the LORD, for his mercy is very great; but do not let me fall into human hands" (1 Chronicles 21:13).

Wise choice. If you want grace, fall into the hands of God. If you want judgment, fall into the hands of fellow human beings. David knows that. He makes the best choice. "I'll take three days of the sword of the Lord," says David. But even that is horrible to endure. Those who are under David's leadership will be the ones who have to pay the price for his punishment. How miserable David must feel, knowing *his* failure will cause *their* pain and loss.

A pathetic scene follows as David sees the movement of God's scythe across the land of Israel, cutting people down, one after another. It's beyond description, this horrific loss of life caused by his own act of foolishness: "The LORD sent a plague on Israel from that morning until the end of the time designated, and seventy thousand of the people from Dan to Beersheba died" (2 Samuel 24:15).

The plague in time reaches fully close to home: "God sent an angel to destroy Jerusalem" (1 Chronicles 21:15). Jerusalem! Think of it: God is going to destroy this great capital city—David's city.

> But as the angel was doing so, the LORD saw it and relented concerning the disaster and said to the angel who was destroying the people, "Enough! Withdraw your hand."
> The angel of the LORD was then standing at the threshing floor of Araunah the Jebusite. (1 Chronicles 21:15)

The king has been watching the carnage:

> David looked up and saw the angel of the LORD standing between heaven and earth, with a drawn sword in his hand extended over Jerusalem. Then David and the elders, clothed in sackcloth, fell facedown.
> David said to God, "Was it not I who ordered the fighting men to be counted? I, the shepherd, have sinned and done wrong. These are but sheep. What have they done? LORD my God, let your hand fall on me and my family, but do not let this plague remain on your people." (1 Chronicles 21:16–17)

Sin pays a terrible wage. Those who've been raised in church have heard that so long and so often that it no longer has much impact. But it should!

Sin demands a payment, and David sees the crushing, incredible immensity of it. He sees sin's ugliness, sin's devastation, sin's horror. David is a broken man facing the responsibility of his own iniquity, and he throws himself upon the mercy of God.

The Lord answers by revealing the first step in a long-term plan here: "Then the angel of the LORD ordered Gad to tell David to go up and build an altar to the LORD on the threshing floor of Araunah the Jebusite" (1 Chronicles 21:18).

It's amazing how obedient one becomes after suffering sin's terrible consequences. There was no hesitation on David's part, not a single question asked. David in this moment will go anywhere and do anything God requires.

> So David went up in obedience to the word that Gad had spoken in the name of the LORD.

> While Araunah was threshing wheat, he turned and saw the angel;
> his four sons who were with him hid themselves.
>
> Then David approached, and when Araunah looked and saw him,
> he left the threshing floor and bowed down before David with his face to
> the ground. (1 Chronicles 21:19–21)

David's sin that was involved in commanding the census is not public knowledge. This man Araunah (also known as Ornan) still sees his king as a man of God. That's part of the peril of spiritual leadership; people often think only the best as they put leaders on a pedestal. David here could take advantage of this, but he knows only too well the dark side of his own life. And in spite of all the faults and blunders in his life, he is still a man after God's heart.

To get the full picture of this encounter with Gad, let's look at the parallel passage in 2 Samuel:

> So David went up, as the LORD had commanded through Gad. When
> Araunah looked and saw the king and his officials coming toward him,
> he went out and bowed down before the king with his face to the ground.
>
> Araunah said, "Why has my lord the king come to his servant?"
>
> "To buy your threshing floor," David answered, "so I can build an
> altar to the LORD, that the plague on the people may be stopped."
>
> Araunah said to David, "Let my lord the king take whatever he
> wishes and offer it up. Here are oxen for the burnt offering, and here are
> threshing sledges and ox yokes for the wood. Your Majesty, Araunah gives
> all this to the king." Araunah also said to him, "May the LORD your God
> accept you." (24:19–23)

Little did Araunah realize the sinfulness of his king's life. In childlike innocence, this man felt honored to let David have anything he owned. What trust, what respect! How it must have pained David to hear those words. Broken, and knowing the ugly truth of his own life, he is able by the grace of God to stand there and reject this man's offer.

> But the king replied to Araunah, "No, I insist on paying you for it. I will
> not sacrifice to the LORD my God burnt offerings that cost me nothing."

> So David bought the threshing floor and the oxen and paid fifty
> shekels of silver for them. (24:24)

David says he can't take as a gift what the man offers; he is morally
bound to pay for it. So David buys the land and the oxen, and he constructs
the altar where God has commanded:

> David built an altar to the LORD there and sacrificed burnt offerings and
> fellowship offerings. Then the LORD answered his prayer in behalf of the
> land, and the plague on Israel was stopped. (24:25)

And we get this awe-inducing picture: "The LORD spoke to the angel,
and he put his sword back into its sheath" (1 Chronicles 21:27). With
David's obedience, the pestilence—the plague—is over. What a relief to
read that the angel's sword is put away. The scent of David's offering is a
sweet fragrance in heaven—and the Lord has determined that the enacted
judgment is enough. What grace!

WARNINGS FOR TODAY

Reading about this deathly plague sent as judgment for David's sin, you may
be thinking, *How can God do such things?* Frankly, my question instead is
this: "How can God stop where He does, knowing what we deserve?" We
deserve *none* of the benefits that come our way; they're all benefits of His
magnificent grace. If sinful folks like us got what we really "deserved," it
would be nothing short of death and hell itself.

Though David has assurance that the sword is back in its sheath, there
were still seventy thousand fresh graves in Israel. There are thousands of
grieving families whose lives are painfully marked by David's compromise
with pride.

Every spiritual leader would do well to read this story once a year!

David's experience offers us three warnings.

1. *To live an unaccountable life is to flirt with danger.* Accountability is
one of the things God uses to keep His people pure. We all need to be held

accountable by someone. If David had listened to Joab, he would never have numbered the people, or been the cause of such devastation.

2. *To ignore sin's consequences is to reject God's truth.* The Bible is filled with the reality of sin's consequences. Sin is a selfish act meant to bring ourselves pleasure, with little care about the toll it takes on others.

3. *To fail to take God seriously is to deny His lordship.* In the midst of the enjoyable fun and delight of living—and no one believes in that more than I do—it's tempting to go too far and take the edge off God's holiness. Why take ourselves so seriously? But when it comes to God, we need to take Him *very* seriously, and not play games. And when we do take Him seriously, He gives us the delight and satisfaction of a full life.

I believe if somehow we could bring David back from beyond and interview him today, one of his strongest pieces of advice would be directed toward spiritual leaders—those who've earned people's respect and trust. I think he would speak from his own experience and urgently warn against falling under the subtle spell of pride.

If a man as great and godly as David could foul up his life at such great cost, so near the end—then so can anyone. So can you or I. God help us all.

———————

GOING AFTER GOD'S OWN HEART: From David's Psalm 25, make his prayer your own:

> Turn to me and be gracious to me,
> for I am lonely and afflicted.
> Relieve the troubles of my heart
> and free me from my anguish.
> Look on my affliction and my distress
> and take away all my sins. (25:16–18)

CHAPTER 24

END OF AN ERA

The death of David, the greatest king Israel ever had, marked the closing of a time period on earth that could never be duplicated. As great a king as David's son Solomon would become, he never took the place or equaled the reign of his father. In a real sense, David both began and ended an era.

I suppose we would say God broke the mold after He made David.

G. Frederick Owen called David's reign "the most successful royal career recorded in the annals of history," as he splendidly summarized a few highlights:

> David satisfied the people throughout Israel, quieted the Philistines for all time to come, then in the midst of peace and plenty he wrote many psalms of praise to Jehovah. The elderly king gathered vast stores of stone, iron, brass, and cedar for the erection of the temple of God, [and] gave his parting charge.[27]

In the New Testament, in the first sermon we have from the apostle Paul, he stated that death for this great king did not come until "David had served God's purpose in his own generation" (Acts 13:36).

Will it be possible to make that statement about you and me? That we served the purpose of God in our own generation, before passing from this earth?

Each of us has a purpose for living. Not many have a purpose so great and prominent as David's, but everyone God brings to life on this earth is significant. The tragedy of all tragedies is that we should live and die without having found our purpose—that special, God-ordained reason for serving our generation.

You have unique contributions to make to your generation; in that sense (among others), you're like no other person on this planet. Those contributions may not exactly match your dreams; they might even be far beyond your wildest expectations. But whatever they are, you're to find them and carry them out. And then, when your twilight years go by and your life is ended, you can be satisfied that you've served God's purpose with your life.

David's purpose was to serve as a king and to perpetuate the righteousness of Israel. In 1 Chronicles 28 and 29, we find the narrative of his life's end, as well as his last recorded words. In the closing chapter of his years on earth, David is particularly involved in three activities: (1) preparations for the building and functioning of the temple in Jerusalem; (2) giving guidance to Solomon, his son and royal heir; and (3) praying before the Lord while rejoicing with the assembly of the people of Israel. After carrying out these significant activities, Israel's greatest king died—ending an era.

AN UNFULFILLED DREAM

After his decades of service to Israel, David was old and perhaps stooped by the years as he looked for the last time into the faces of his trusted followers:

> David summoned all the officials of Israel to assemble at Jerusalem: the officers over the tribes, the commanders of the divisions in the service of the king, the commanders of thousands and commanders of hundreds, and the officials in charge of all the property and livestock belonging to the king and his sons, together with the palace officials, the warriors and all the brave fighting men. (1 Chronicles 28:1)

What an awesome gathering this is! The group probably numbers in the hundreds. Each face represents a memory in the old man's mind. Here they all are, surrounding their beloved and aged king, who will give them the parting words of his life.

"King David rose to his feet" (28:1). Perhaps he lifts his hand to quiet the assembly, and his voice quivers as he begins:

> "Listen to me, my fellow Israelites, my people. I had it in my heart to build a house as a place of rest for the ark of the covenant of the LORD, for the footstool of our God, and I made plans to build it." (28:2)

Reading this verse, I can feel the immediacy of the truth of this long-past dream in David's life. He has lived and will die with a frustrated desire—building the temple of God was the single legacy David desired most.

I feel the immediacy in both the words and the spirit of this verse because I know that beating in the heart of every thinking person there's a dream, a desire. When we're able to be absolutely honest with ourselves before God, you and I entertain certain dreams, certain hopes.

Think about it. By the end of your days, what you want above all things to have accomplished is: _____ (you fill in the blank). That's your own personal desire, your secret dream. However, on the basis of David's experience, I must say it's quite possible that you'll die with that desire unfulfilled. This may be one of the hardest things in life for you to face and accept.

David faces this reality as a man after God's own heart. What a remarkable person! He has this deep desire to build the temple, to which the Lord's answer was no—and David's response is acceptance. He has heard the Lord's no, and he doesn't resent it. "But God said to me, 'You are not to build a house for my Name, because you are a warrior and have shed blood'" (28:3).

When Solomon was born, he was given the name that means "peace." *Shalom*, the familiar Hebrew term known all around the world, is directly related in root form to the name Solomon. So the Lord chose David's son—a peacemaker and diplomat, not a man of war—to build His house. He wanted a man of a different temperament than David to fulfill that dream. David recognizes this and has quietly accepted God's no.

For most of us, that's awfully hard to do. Dreams die hard. But look further at David's response:

"Yet the LORD, the God of Israel, chose me from my whole family to be king over Israel forever. He chose Judah as leader, and from the tribe of Judah he chose my family, and from my father's sons he was pleased to make me king over all Israel." (28:4)

David here is focusing on what God *has* allowed him to do, rather than pining away over this unfulfilled desire. It's easy for us to be so disappointed and distraught over a frustrated desire that we forget the many good things God has given us and accomplished through our efforts. But not David! I exclaim once again: What a man! He's truly able to look at life from God's point of view.

Look at how positively he reviews God's plan in his life as he continues speaking to this gathering of Israel's leaders:

"Of all my sons—and the LORD has given me many—he has chosen my son Solomon to sit on the throne of the kingdom of the LORD over Israel. He said to me: 'Solomon your son is the one who will build my house and my courts, for I have chosen him to be my son, and I will be his father. I will establish his kingdom forever if he is unswerving in carrying out my commands and laws, as is being done at this time.'

"So now I charge you in the sight of all Israel and of the assembly of the LORD, and in the hearing of our God: Be careful to follow all the commands of the LORD your God, that you may possess this good land and pass it on as an inheritance to your descendants forever." (28:5–8)

David is saying, "When it came to my own dream, God answered no, not yes. But He has given me other things in place of that dream, and I'm making the very most them!" We can all glean much from David's wholesome response.

Do you have some cherished desire that you know you'll have to relinquish? Usually it takes getting on up in years to realize that's going to happen, because the younger we are, the greater our dreams, the broader our hopes, and the more determined we are to make them happen. As we get older, many of us see that some of those great hopes and dreams will never be realized. Perhaps it's a dream of some great accomplishment through a unique kind of ministry. Maybe it's a desire for a certain kind of career or recognition. Maybe it's a desire for romance and marriage. Maybe it's a hope for relief from some burden or disadvantage in your life that you've had to live with for years. Whatever it is, you may now recognize that your dream will never happen—and this is a hard pill to swallow. But it's also an opportunity for you, like David, to find satisfaction in what God has allowed you to experience and achieve. You turn your attention away from what is not to be, and you focus on where God has clearly been at work in your life.

Some live their last years of life being swamped by guilt or overwhelmed by past failures. But others can say, "By the grace of God, I did the best I could with what I had. And I claim His promise that somehow He'll use what I did accomplish for His greater glory." What a wonderful attitude to have at the end of one's life!

A SON UNTRIED

In an emotional moment, David turns now and looks at his son Solomon. He smiles as he sees in that young man the possibility of his long-awaited dream being fulfilled. David won't experience it himself—but his son will. So he passes on advice to his son.

David carefully chooses these parting words. They're measured words, based on his experience over the years as king. His words are full of emotion, rich with meaning, as he looks back over forty years as Israel's leader. He speaks slowly and carefully:

> "And you, my son Solomon, acknowledge the God of your father, and serve him with wholehearted devotion and with a willing mind, for the LORD searches every heart and understands every desire and every thought." (28:9)

Not surprisingly, these words from David to his son have to do with godliness. "Know the Lord," David is saying. "Know the God of your father." David is aware of the tyranny of the urgent. From his four tumultuous decades as king of Israel, he knows that for anyone on that throne, there's enough to keep a man so busy he'll be tempted not to take time to know God. "Above all things, Solomon, I want you to *know God*."

Before you die, what's the most important piece of advice regarding life that you would want to pass on to those you love most? And what advice are you passing on right now? What character and lifestyle are you investing in others around you?

David looks deeply into the eyes of his beloved son Solomon, this son of grace from David's union with Bathsheba. I wonder if David sees in this young man the early markings of waywardness and loose living that Solomon experiences later. As the king thinks back on mistakes in his own life, he may be especially concerned that those patterns don't repeat in his son's life. So David says, "Know God, my son. Above all else, get to know Him deeply, intimately."

David also speaks to Solomon here of serving God in the profoundly best way: "with wholehearted devotion and with a willing mind." David spells that out. "Solomon, don't make God force you to worship Him. Do it wholeheartedly. Do it willingly. Hold nothing back."

David can say those things because that's the kind of heart he has. He's the sweet singer of Israel who has composed and sung these great songs of praise to the Lord, and Solomon knows this. Solomon certainly has witnessed in his father an intense passion for God. His dad's devotion would be an unforgettable legacy in Solomon's mind.

What is your own spiritual legacy? If you're a parent, will your children grow up knowing that you served the Lord God willingly, with a whole heart? Are you modeling that for them in your life? There's no better teaching tool in the life of a child than the model of a parent's life surrendered to the Lord God.

David can admonish Solomon to serve God willingly and wholeheartedly because David himself has done this. Not perfectly, of course. In fact, he reminds Solomon that "the LORD searches every heart and understands every desire and every thought." In saying that, David can recall the dark day years before when he stayed home from battle and fell into sin. He may be thinking, *Solomon, don't fall in those ways as I did.*

Then David says more to Solomon about seeking God and fulfilling the Lord's calling on his life:

"If you seek him, he will be found by you; but if you forsake him, he will reject you forever. Consider now, for the LORD has chosen you to build a house as the sanctuary. Be strong and do the work." (28:9–10)

David goes on to speak about constructing the temple. It's as if he pulls Solomon aside and says, "Now look, son, I've got all these plans laid out." Maybe he even unrolls the project's drawings, and these two men get down on their hands and knees together:

Then David gave his son Solomon the plans for the portico of the temple, its buildings, its storerooms, its upper parts, its inner rooms, and the place of atonement. He gave him the plans of all that the Spirit had put in his mind for the courts of the temple of the LORD and all the surrounding rooms, for the treasuries of the temple of God and for the treasuries for the dedicated things. (28:11–12)

This grand temple is David's dream, and he's saying, "Solomon, if you're going build it, build it right. And this is how." Room by room by room, he lays it out. Doesn't that sound like a dad? What a model of diligence, alertness, and keen perception David is in all this. What a heritage for Solomon to build on.

The king sends more encouragement Solomon's way:

David also said to Solomon his son, "Be strong and courageous, and do the work. Do not be afraid or discouraged, for the LORD God, my God, is with you. He will not fail you or forsake you until all the work for the service of the temple of the LORD is finished." (28:20)

Perhaps he mentions fear and discouragement because David knows only too well the problems Solomon will encounter as a political ruler, which will be Solomon's primary calling and career. David might be hinting, "With your every decision and action as king, there'll be lots of pressure—you'll have plenty of people on one side, and plenty of others on the opposite side. So walk closely with God—He'll be right there with you all the way."

The next words are for all the people:

Then King David said to the whole assembly: "My son Solomon, the one whom God has chosen, is young and inexperienced. The task is great, because this palatial structure is not for man but for the LORD God." (29:1)

I can picture Solomon standing there, with his heart pounding in his throat. He's young, inexperienced, untried. And there stands his battle-scarred father, after forty incomparably momentous years as king, handing over the scepter of Israel and the plans for the temple of God. His face is wrinkled with age, but those dark eyes are flashing with excitement. What a moment! What a father!

Solomon will enjoy numerous benefits because of David's exceptional accomplishments. Let me give you a list. The nation is now unified under one ruler. A royal capital had been established in Jerusalem. The military forces of Israel are now respected by enemies around them, and they've all been subdued, including the Philistines. Israel's area has been extended from six thousand square miles to sixty thousand. Prosperity has been brought in by the extensive trade routes David has set up. The people hunger for God and righteousness, and the sounds of David's songs can be heard throughout the land.

I'd call all that an enviable legacy—and it was Solomon's to enjoy. If any son ever had reason to be grateful, this one does.

One of the tendencies of any new generation is ingratitude toward those who came before. How seldom we express our gratitude to our parents and their peers for all they've invested in our lives. And yet we soak up the benefits of their dedicated labors. May God make us more thankful, especially if we've had parents whose lives paved the way for our walk with God—and even more so if they invested their time and treasure in us!

THE LORD, AN UNCHANGING FATHER

At the end of this scene, David falls on his knees and utters a beautiful prayer, an extemporaneous expression of his worship of the Lord God. The first verses are expressions of praise. True praise of the Lord leaves humanity out of the picture and focuses fully on exalting the living God. The magnifying glass looks up. David does this with great feeling:

David praised the LORD in the presence of the whole assembly, saying,

> "Praise be to you, LORD,
> the God of our father Israel,
> from everlasting to everlasting.
> Yours, LORD, is the greatness and the power
> and the glory and the majesty and the splendor,
> for everything in heaven and earth is yours.
> Yours, LORD, is the kingdom;
> you are exalted as head over all.
> Wealth and honor come from you;
> you are the ruler of all things.
> In your hands are strength and power
> to exalt and give strength to all.
> Now, our God, we give you thanks,
> and praise your glorious name." (1 Chronicles 29:10–13)

With overflowing gratitude in his heart, David moves spontaneously into thanksgiving for all that God has done throughout the years of his life, and especially for the people's willing and abundant contributions for the temple's construction:

"Now, our God, we give you thanks, and praise your glorious name. But who am I, and who are my people, that we should be able to give as generously as this? Everything comes from you, and we have given you only what comes from your hand. We are foreigners and strangers in your sight, as were all our ancestors. Our days on earth are like a shadow, without hope. Lord our God, all this abundance that we have provided for building you a temple for your Holy Name comes from your hand, and all of it belongs to you.

"I know, my God, that you test the heart and are pleased with integrity. All these things I have given willingly and with honest intent. And now I have seen with joy how willingly your people who are here have given to you." (29:13–17)

Now there you have a proper scale of values! David is surrounded by limitless riches, yet these have never captured his heart. He has fought other battles within, but never greed. David isn't trapped by materialism. He says, "Lord, everything we have is Yours—all these beautiful places where we gather for worship, the place where I live, the throne room—all of it is Yours, everything." David holds everything loosely.

A proper scale of values is such an important investment to instill in our children and all those we influence. They need to know how to handle the good things of life, and to realize that material things are here today and gone tomorrow. They must also learn how to handle life and our possessions and surroundings when things aren't easy.

David now intercedes for the people he has ruled for forty years, and once again for his son:

"LORD, the God of our fathers Abraham, Isaac and Israel, keep these desires and thoughts in the hearts of your people forever, and keep their hearts loyal to you. And give my son Solomon the wholehearted devotion to keep your commands, statutes and decrees and to do everything to build the palatial structure for which I have provided."

Then David said to the whole assembly, "Praise the LORD your God." (29:18–20)

Praising God is precisely what the people do—spontaneously, in response to David's prayer:

So they all praised the LORD, the God of their fathers; they bowed down, prostrating themselves before the LORD and the king. (29:20)

What a moment this is! Though it's the end of an era, it doesn't lead to sadness and mourning and grief, but to gladness and rejoicing before God.

The next day they made sacrifices to the LORD and presented burnt offerings to him: a thousand bulls, a thousand rams and a thousand male lambs, together with their drink offerings, and other sacrifices in abundance for all Israel. They ate and drank with great joy in the presence of the LORD that day. Then they acknowledged Solomon son of David as king . . . anointing him before the LORD to be ruler. (29:21–22)

Through the valor and grace, and the wisdom and faithfulness of his father David, Solomon is off to a great start as king:

So Solomon sat on the throne of the LORD as king in place of his father David. He prospered and all Israel obeyed him. All the officers and warriors, as well as all of King David's sons, pledged their submission to King Solomon.

The LORD highly exalted Solomon in the sight of all Israel and bestowed on him royal splendor such as no king over Israel ever had before. (29:23–25)

We can be assured that no one was more thrilled with Solomon's good start than his father, David, whose time to leave this world has come: "He died at a good old age, having enjoyed long life, wealth and honor" (29:28).

Now there's an epitaph to be pleased with! Good for you, David!

When a man of God dies, nothing of God dies. And when a man of God dies, none of God's principles die. Nowhere is that seen more clearly than in the life of David.

What lessons can we learn from such a man? Here are good places to look for them:

- David's hope in God, despite his human failings.
- David's courage in the midst of his own fear.
- David's encouragement in the Lord, and his praise and thanksgiving to Him, as expressed in the songs growing out of his hours of despair.
- David's experience of the Lord's forgiveness for his dark moments of sin.
- David's commitment to serve the purpose of God in his own generation, despite all his dreams not being fulfilled.

Thank you, David!—for being our model, teaching us by your life such significant truths!

And thank You, Father, for being our Master; using us though we are weak, forgiving us when we fail, and loving us through all the ordeals of our lives. Thank You for showing us that we can be people like David—people of valor and grace, people of passion and destiny.

GOING AFTER GOD'S OWN HEART: From David's Psalm 86, make his prayer your own:

> Teach me your way, LORD,
> that I may rely on your faithfulness;
> give me an undivided heart,
> that I may fear your name.
> I will praise you, Lord my God, with all my heart;
> I will glorify your name forever.
> For great is your love toward me;
> you have delivered me from the depths,
> from the realm of the dead. (86:11–13)

NOTES

1. George Frederick Owen, *Abraham to the Middle-East Crisis* (Eerdmans, 1939, 1957), 45.
2. Attributed to British pastor, evangelist, and author Alan Redpath (1907–1989).
3. F. B. Meyer, *David: Shepherd, Psalmist, King* (Christian Literature Crusade, 1977), 18.
4. C. F. Keil and F. Delitzsch, *Commentary on the Old Testament*, vol. 2 (Eerdmans, 1960), 170.
5. C. H. Spurgeon, *The Treasury of David*, in eight volumes, published consecutively between 1865 and 1885.
6. G. Campbell Morgan, *The Unfolding Message of the Bible* (Fleming H. Revell Co., 1961), 232.
7. Lawrence O. Richards, entry for "Understand/Understanding" in *Zondervan Expository Dictionary of Bible Words* (Zondervan, 1985, 1991), 604.
8. H. G. Wells, *The History of Mr. Polly* (The Press of the Reader's Club, 1941), 5.
9. Wayne Dyer, *Your Erroneous Zones* (Avon Books, 1976), 218–19.
10. Alan Redpath, *The Making of a Man of God* (Fleming H. Revell Co., 1962), 107.
11. Rollo May, *Love and Will* (W. W. Norton and Co., 1969), 15.
12. F. B. Meyer, *Christ in Isaiah* (Christian Literature Crusade, nd), 9.
13. Owen, *Abraham to the Middle-East Crisis*, 5.
14. J. Oswald Sanders, *Robust in Faith* (Moody Press 1965), 121.
15. C. S. Lewis, *Screwtape Letters* (Collier Books, Macmillan, 1959), 132.
16. Dietrich Bonhoeffer, *Temptation* (Macmillan, 1953), 116–17.
17. Meyer, *David*, 195.

18. Paul Tournier, *Guilt and Grace* (Harper & Row, 1958), 97.

19. Alexander Whyte, *Bible Characters* (Zondervan, 1952), 245.

20. John W. Lawrence, *Life's Choices* (Multnomah Press, 1975), 39.

21. Whyte, *Bible Characters*, 309.

22. Samuel Taylor Coleridge, "Youth and Age," as published in *Poems That Live Forever*, selected by Hazel Felleman (Doubleday, 1965), 256.

23. *The NIV Study Bible*, Kenneth Barker, ed. (Zondervan, 1985), 447.

24. Samuel Johnson, cited in *John Bartlett's Familiar Quotations*, ed. Emily Morison Beck (Little Brown, and Co., 1980), 354.

25. Whyte, *Bible Characters*, 297.

26. J. Oswald Sanders, *Spiritual Leadership,* revised edition(Moody Press, 2007, 2017), 139.

27. Owen, *Abraham to the Middle-East Crisis*, 54.

ABOUT THE AUTHOR

Pastor Charles R. Swindoll has devoted his life to the accurate, practical teaching and application of God's Word. He is the founding pastor of Stonebriar Community Church in Frisco, Texas, but Chuck's listening audience extends far beyond a local church body. As a leading program in Christian broadcasting since 1979, *Insight for Living* airs around the world, carrying Chuck's Bible-teaching content to spiritually hungry hearts in numerous nations. Chuck's leadership as president and now chancellor emeritus at Dallas Theological Seminary has helped prepare and equip a new generation of men and women for ministry.